CW00972219

A RO

ALSO BY DAVID KING DUNAWAY

Jungle Sea: Poems and Translations

Oral History: An Interdisciplinary Anthology

Writing the Southwest

Huxley in Hollywood

Aldous Huxley Recollected: An Oral History

Across the Tracks: A Route 66 Story

How Can I Keep from Singing? The Ballad of Pete Seeger

Singing Out: An Oral History of America's Folk Music Revivals

A Pete Seeger Discography

A ROUTE 66 Companion

EDITED BY
DAVID KING DUNAWAY

FOREWORD BY
MICHAEL WALLIS

ILLUSTRATIONS BY
BOB WALDMIRE

UNIVERSITY OF TEXAS PRESS
AUSTIN

Copyright © 2012 by David King Dunaway
All rights reserved
Printed in the United States of America
First edition, 2012

Illustrated map and postcards of Route 66 by Bob Waldmire, © 1992. Courtesy of
Buz Waldmire.

Requests for permission to reproduce material from this work should be sent to:
    Permissions
    University of Texas Press
    P.O. Box 7819
    Austin, TX 78713-7819
    www.utexas.edu/utpress/about/bpermission.html

♾ The paper used in this book meets the minimum requirements of ANSI/NISO
Z39.48-1992 (R1997) (Permanence of Paper).

LIBRARY OF CONGRESS CATALOGING-IN-PUBLICATION DATA

    A Route 66 companion / edited by David King Dunaway ; foreword by Michael
Wallis ; illustrations by Robert Waldmire. — 1st ed.
        p.   cm.
    Includes bibliographical references.
    ISBN 978-0-292-72660-4 (cloth : alk. paper) — ISBN 978-0-292-73573-6 (e-book)
    1. United States Highway 66—Literary collections.   I. Dunaway, David King.
II. Waldmire, Robert.
    PS648.U55R68   2012
    810.9'35873—dc23
                                                2011032482

CONTENTS

FOREWORD: **AMERICA'S ROAD**

MICHAEL WALLIS

R oute 66 is the most famous highway in America, and arguably the world. To this day, Route 66 still captures the attention and imagination of legions of travelers, a highway of dreams realized and dreams lost.

Unveiled in 1926, it was only a few years before the highway was on everyone's map. In no time it became "America's Main Street." During the turbulent 1930s, tens of thousands of tenant farmers, Okies, Arkies, and other desperate refugees from the Midwest and southern Plains took to the highway. Eager to rebuild their shattered lives, they followed the scent of orange blossoms to California, the so-called promised land.

During World War II, troops trained along the entire length of the highway and convoys motored east and west. Then, at the close of the war, Route 66 experienced what many consider its glory years. America's passionate love affair with the internal combustion engine increased and big gas-guzzling cars with fins became the rage, just as President Dwight Eisenhower changed everything with a single stroke of his pen. On June 29, 1956, he sent America speeding down an off-ramp toward the future of an automobile-oriented society. In signing the Federal-Aid Highway Act, which created the nation's interstate highway system, Eisenhower not only made Route 66 obsolete, he kick-started a nationwide freeway-construction boom.

The result of that single act literally rearranged the way people live their lives in America. One road expert pointed out that the amount of concrete used to build the network could erect a wall nine feet thick and fifty feet high around the world. The interstate highway system that resulted was undoubtedly the most important and grandest public works project in United States history.

True enough, the interstate boom brought an economic boom, driving the growth of fast-food outlets, national motel chains, and other cookie-cutter businesses built around off-ramps.

The interstate network also brought urban sprawl. With the creation of the new highways, it became possible for people to live a significant distance from their workplaces. This new-found ease of travel lured residents and businesses from city centers, leading to the decline of many downtowns and creating communities that required driving to get to the supermarket, the park, school, church, and, of course, the shopping mall. Some politicians and big business interests called it "progress."

In the long run, the Interstate Highway System, for all its supposed virtues, may well be seen as a mistake. At least, that is what a growing number of Route 66 proponents came to believe. They speculated on what the United States might have become had it invested earlier in improving the railroads or developing better ways of moving people. Yet even as the familiar Route 66 shield signs were removed and road maps changed, these people knew that Route 66 would never die. Their ranks soon swelled and continue to grow today. They are the protectors of pop culture, the commercial archaeologists, preservationists, and historians who joined forces with the folks who still eke out a living along the old highway. Together they ignited the intense revival of interest in Route 66 that still gains momentum. If Route 66 is to have any kind of future, the past must be acknowledged.

That is precisely why *A Route 66 Companion*, compiled by David King Dunaway, is so important. This collection of historic narratives, prose, poetry, essays, and personal memories provides readers with the most comprehensive view ever offered of the greater Route 66 story. Dunaway, however, does not present the romanticized viewpoint of the Mother Road—past and present—that often ignores reality. He goes much further, and in so doing validates the entire experience of open-road travel. For that reason alone I consider Dunaway's anthology one of the most important contributions to the ongoing effort to preserve and protect Route 66.

For we have always been a restless people. Long before any white intruders came to the continent, Native Americans kept on the go. They moved from place to place to avoid inclement weather, follow the great herds of bison, or escape warring tribes. They carved a network of trails and traces later used by white explorers and settlers. Some of those same pathways eventually became the foundation of many of our existing paved highways, including Route 66.

By reading about the time before there was a highway, we can better understand our own history and learn from it. All we have to do is go back to a time long ago. Back to bedrock. To those who knew the land in its natural state. Go back and imagine—dare to imagine. Route 66 has always been a place where people are free to imagine. Imagine when there were no roads or highways. No cities, towns, farms, or factories. Imagine no boundaries or borders. Imagine a time when the prairies and stands of trees were the churches, temples, and cathedrals. Imagine no prisons, cemeteries, country clubs, casinos, or shopping malls. Imagine when there were no cars or trucks.

And then go back to when the first cars did appear. Go back to when Route 66 was a new road—parts of it unscarred, unproven, unknown, and unpaved. Back to bold days when crews of men and mules and machines carved new roadbed. When dreamers connected stretches of existing highways. When the road became a linear village. Back to when Cyrus Avery was the newly crowned Father of Route 66 and when Andrew Hartley Payne pulled on his racing singlet and prepared to run in the 1928 "Bunion Derby," the Great Transcontinental Footrace.

Go back before the coming of the networks of interstate highways— those super slabs of monotony that now crisscross the land. Go back to the hot, sad days and agonizing nights of the Great Depression and the devastating Dust Bowl. Back to when an entire nation's life was interrupted first by acts of God and then, a few years later, by acts of madmen, when the world went to war. Back to when people of color could not find the comfort afforded white travelers on the Mother Road.

Go back to when there were no strip centers or shopping malls. When there were no Golden Arches, Starbucks, or Walmart. Go back to when gasoline was dirt cheap and a ten-dollar bill—maybe even five bucks—got you through a Friday night date just fine. When there was no bottled water, no credit cards, no cappuccino, and no cholesterol.

Imagine a time when no one locked doors, when there was no air-conditioning or television, and when everyone sat on the front porch. People actually looked each other in the eye, had conversations, wrote long and beautiful letters by hand, and mailed home postcards. No text messaging, cell phones, or Internet.

Hitchhiking was safe for both parties, and drive-in movies were not on the endangered species list. There were genuine waitresses and real carhops. Food tasted better. Summer lasted longer.

Go back and then imagine the old highway—this road I love—as it was, as it now is, and as it will become. This crooked path littered with history, aspirations, broken promises, and fulfilled dreams has been shaped by its geography.

Route 66 is big cities and tiny towns. It is rich farmland, Ozark forests, vast prairies and rangeland, high and low desert, great mountains, mighty streams. Flood, earthquake, fire, and killer tornadoes have tempered it and its people. Route 66 is the eight states it traverses and bits and pieces of forty-two more. It is American, through and through.

The highway has yielded plenty of saints and a good many sinners. It is not just black and white, but shades of gray and all the colors of the rainbow and then some.

The Route 66 story is both bitter and sweet. A microcosm of the nation, the old road has plenty of scar tissue, much to be ashamed of and much to brag about, as well as a bright future. It is an unfinished story—a work in progress. It always will be.

INTRODUCTION

Route 66 has always represented big ideas to America and to the world: a chance to start over, a road to a better life. In its wake from Los Angeles to Chicago, it encompasses two-thirds of a continent and perhaps one-quarter of the U.S. population.

To many who traveled Route 66, it represents the good ol' days of their youth, ripe with nostalgia and innocent illusions. Looking backward, Route 66 is seen by many as the epitome of America at its golden age, midway through the American century. Cars were sleek, gas cheap, the road open; anything could happen there. Route 66 was footloose guys in a cool Corvette having adventures at every stop on a television series. Route 66 was a set of movies and songs about escaping the Dust Bowl. For Europeans, Route 66 was the freedom to travel thousands of miles on the same road and to never be asked what you're doing there. Route 66 was the road you got your kicks on and the road to California, which shimmered like paradise with a tropical view.

Route 66 has been a road for all America, not just the Midwest and Southwest and California, where it passes. But it's not just a road for Americans; there are books about it in Japanese, Swedish, German, and Brazilian Portuguese. This volume contains clues as to why a road attracts so many visitors from different continents.

Recently, the Old Road—decommissioned but mostly still drivable—has turned 85. Angel Delgadillo, a barber on Arizona's Route 66, has watched European tourists actually climb down off their bus and kiss the pavement, saying, "This is the true America."

A comprehensive, thoughtful look at Route 66 is long overdue. U.S. Highway 66 is among America's glory roads, alongside the Boston Post Road, the Lincoln Highway, and California's Route 1. As John Steinbeck wrote in *The Grapes of Wrath* (1939):

> Highway 66 is the main migrant road, 66—the long concrete path across the country, waving gently up and down on the map. . . . 66 is the mother road, the road of flight.

Steinbeck understood the deep tie between this highway and the great American myths of freedom and starting over. He captured the essence of Route 66 during the Depression, but this corridor is far older than that, assembled from transits dating back to buffalo trails and the native hunters who followed them along the banks of the South Canadian River. In Illinois, U.S. 66 followed trails of Indians migrating from Lake Michigan to the Mississippi (Dodge 1980). Westward from what would be St. Louis, trails (and later, the National Old Trails Highways) rotated westward from Cahokia, the largest pre-Columbian Indian settlement in the Midwest. These paralleled the Fort Smith, Arkansas, wagon road and the New Mexican portions of the Santa Fe Trail across canyons and mountain passes. Later, following the railroad crossings, the first muddy roads dragged through a wilderness of plains and forests. People with a stake in movement followed: homesteaders, miners, railroad builders.

By the mid-nineteenth century, the national expansion of railways opened another chapter in the history of what would be Route 66. After nineteenth-century surveys of Edward Beale and others, railroads (on the congressional land grants they were given) created a steel trail joining the Pacific Coast to the Midwest. They crossed some of the most inhospitable reaches in U.S. geography: Texas's gumbo mud and the vast Mojave Desert, which required water tanks every ten miles for steam engines. The list of companies laying the grade for what would be Route 66 is long; a partial list (from west to east): the Atlantic and Pacific; the Atchison, Topeka and Santa Fe; the Rock Island; the Texas and Pacific; St. Louis–San Francisco (also called the Frisco); and the Illinois Central, among more than a dozen. The railroads, variously linked, graded the way. Their water stops became towns on 66, and after World War II they ceded freight and passengers to the new road (Waters 1950; Goddard 1994; Jackson 1964).

The planning for U.S. 66 (originally U.S. 60) began in 1921, following the development of the mass production of automobiles and the Good Roads Movement. Originally planned to follow the Santa Fe Trail across Nebraska and Colorado, Route 66 eventually passed further south and east along the thirty-fifth parallel from L.A. to Oklahoma City, before angling north through Tulsa, then east through Missouri and north from St. Louis to Chicago, an "all-weather" route (Riegel 1926; Scott 2000).

In the twenties, Route 66 was largely a farm-to-market road. By the Depression, it had become, in Steinbeck's words, the "migrant road." Incidentally, it introduced travelers to the Southwest and particularly to its native populations. In the forties, Route 66 transported matériel for the war and then hosted returning GIs. In the fifties, trucking companies filled 66's lanes. In Jack Kerouac's *On the Road*, heading west from Chicago took him to Route 66:

> My first ride was a dynamite truck with a red flag, about thirty miles into great green Illinois, the truck driver pointing out the place where Route 6, which we were on, intersects Route 66 before they both shoot west for incredible distances.

By the sixties, the road was so well known—in part from Bobby Troup's popular song, "Get Your Kicks on Route 66"—that it was given its own television series, starring Martin Milner and George Maharis. This brought yet more tourists in the seventies, just as the interstates began to bypass portions of the Old Road. Yet Route 66 is The Road That Wouldn't Die; by 1985, as the government decommissioned it and pulled down signs, preservationists followed in their tracks, putting up historical markers. In our time, and into the future, Route 66 has become a mixed-up symbol of American highways and travel culture and lore (Patton 1986; Krim and Woods 2006).

Route 66 offers a broad avenue into American history, one stratum of road laid down over the other, like the clay tablets that preceded paper and carried traces of older messages. The road's many surfaces (dirt, gravel, poured concrete, macadam) parallel its evolution from paths, trails, rails, to roads. Yesterday's armory is today's senior center; the old gas station becomes a tourist plaza. Route 66 lives on, in popular memory and via oral history. Paradoxically, as with many preservation or revitalization movements, Route 66 really sprung alive after its demise.

Route 66 has been misread as a place of nostalgia for a simpler (read variously: innocent, respectful, rural, segregated) era in the United States. The decades most associated in the popular imagination with Route 66—the 1940s and '50s—are seen as Happy Days, complete with fifties relics: knee socks, Coke bottles, dancing around the jukebox to lyrics less graphic than those listened to by today's teenagers. Yet 66—and its golden era—have another history to tell, one of segregation at bus stops and restaurants and racial profiling of drivers.

For too long, Route 66 has been "whitened," its multicultural past denied. It has been reduced to a set of images fixed in time, small-town nostalgia like Thornton Wilder's *Our Town*, or Garrison Keillor's Lake Wobegon.

With the twenty-first century, a new interpretation of Route 66 has begun, ranging from radio programs and video documentaries to dissertations and serious nonfiction works. From all this, a counter-nostalgic, critical history of Route 66 emerged, replacing with research the hollow shell of Route 66 previously dominated by images of sock hops and malt shops. This "new" history of 66 looks past a triumphalist narrative into the darker corners of what lingers in the American past: the communities and the residents displaced by the building of 66, poverty and injustice, and remaining echoes of racism.

For me, Route 66 is a corridor across time as well as place, an avenue into American history, one broad enough to incorporate all of our westering instincts: a democratic road not just for the traveler, but for those left behind in the dust.

This anthology is an effort to serve up a Route 66 that existed long before U.S. Highway 66 became "Route 66" in bright neon letters. Like 66 itself, this volume contains a great deal for a great many.

For mystery fans it has two all-time greats, Raymond Chandler and Ross MacDonald, and a half-dozen up-and-coming writers. For those who like classic American literature, it includes Washington Irving and John Steinbeck, Henry Miller and Thomas Wolfe.

For those who like their writing with an edge, there's Joan Didion and Rudolfo Anaya; for lovers of the western, Zane Grey and Hal

Evarts, Jr. The America of Route 66 includes tall tales, detective yarns, poetry, and oral histories I conducted—even a radio play that starred Orson Welles. My criteria for inclusion were location and relevance, eloquence and authenticity—writing with a sense of the uniqueness of the Route 66 corridor.

There's living history here from the mouths of those who lived it: miners and ranch hands, migrant workers and tycoons, rock stars and curmudgeons. The interviews took place everywhere, from towns so tiny that maps have lost their name, to fancy hotels in big cities. Here are stories of American Indians born in boxcars on 66, and rocket scientists teaching at Caltech. There's an account of a poor black man who had to buy his sandwich at the back door on 66, and a man who made a wacky monument of Cadillacs stuck face-down into the Texas plains.

There's the history of a man who drove camels across the Continental Divide on what would be Route 66, and the tale of a historian whose tribe was marched to a corral and penned there like cattle. It's the story of the Joads headed down 66 for California, and an account of what happens when some try and go home again. There are stories set in Chicago, St. Louis, Amarillo, Albuquerque, and Hollywood—and many places in between. Each excerpt is a small, tantalizing sample to inspire readers to look at the original work, in its entirety.

This book is organized according to bioregionalism, the theory that the contours of the land and its contents determine the life and culture there. Bioregionalism presupposes an ecological sensitivity: is such a sensitivity the subject of science? Is it basic knowledge or something esoteric, as a generator was to Henry Miller in *The Air-Conditioned Nightmare*? Talking to a Route 66 mechanic in Albuquerque, Miller admitted to "hoping he would first, show me where the damn thing's hidden, and second, that he would tell me whether or not a car could function without one."

To understand the complex intersection of Route 66 and the geography it passes through is a long process of reading ecology. In New Mexico, where I teach at the largest university along 66, Bill DeBuys writes of how mountains and the drainage systems they spawn determine how people live and work together, in a state where water is the most precious commodity. Bioregions, defined through physical and environmental features, have long channeled Route 66's development.

The selections in the anthology are divided into six sections. The first focuses on the prehistory of Route 66. Then, the next four sections are organized geographically, one for each of Route 66's distinct bioregions. A final section peers into 66's future.

The anthology moves east to west, beginning its second section in Illinois, Missouri, and Kansas. The third section, on Oklahoma and Texas, opens with the wit and wisdom of Will Rogers and includes excerpts from *The Grapes of Wrath* and a literary attack on Route 66 by Robert Davis, debunking its myths.

New Mexico and Arizona head up the anthology's fourth section, including stories of Native Americans traveling and living along Route 66, along with Rudolfo Anaya's comic Route 66 encounter: meeting a tourist for the first time.

The fifth section takes us to California with Raymond Chandler, Sylvia Plath, Ross MacDonald, and an oral history by musician Ry Cooder.

The sixth and last section explores possible futures for Route 66, including an interview with a rocket scientist, Aldous Huxley's description of rocket travel along the path of Route 66 in *Brave New World*, and science fiction set in Route 66's Wild West future.

"Route 66 was like your main blood vein going through. Just nothing affected it," Texan writer Delbert Trew said. "All of a sudden you decided to go somewhere—and what did you do? You jump in that main vein and let it take you. And if you come out good, you had a good new life, why then it was the Miracle Road. If it was bad, then it was danged ol' 66 took me there."

Route 66 was a lot more than a road of dreams. Route 66 didn't create racism, but it passed through a great deal of it. It was always a rainbow road, joining communities of color across the country. It was the Indian road to drive without a license while the police patrolled the interstate. It was the Mother Road to towns it nurtured and sustained. Here is its story, from dozens of viewpoints. If Route 66 hadn't existed, America would have had to invent it. And it did.

A ROUTE 66 COMPANION

Three ways of transit along a corridor
that would be Route 66.

①

RAILROADS AND THE
PREHISTORY OF ROUTE 66

BUFFALO HUNTING ON ROUTE 66

DAVE EDMUNDS

– 1840s –

Long before Route 66 was a pretty song or a television series or a way to sell toothpick holders, it was a series of paths, created first by animal crossings and then by the native settlers who followed them. Perhaps the oldest settlement in the Midwest that influenced Route 66 was Cahokia in East St. Louis, near the Mississippi River. Trails radiated out from Cahokia, the largest pre-Columbian settlement in the Midwest, to Ft. Smith and its wagon road, and an early east-west transit emerged.

In a continent bounded by north-south roads, the Canadian River runs east-west, its forks and dry riverbeds snaking their way across the plains. In the nineteenth century, tribes crossed the breaks and fords from the plains of eastern Oklahoma and Missouri to the West, foraging in the creekbeds for water, game, and shelter from the wind. It is here that the story of Route 66 begins, long before railroads drew a hard metal line across the landscape. Dave Edmunds, a Cherokee, is a historian whose compass points towards the public. Professor Edmunds teaches history at the University of Texas at Dallas and has served as the president of the American Society for Ethnohistory and the Western History Association; he is the author of ten volumes of history and more than a hundred articles. He appears as a commentator in television and radio documentaries; his words sit on a plaque at the National Cowboy Hall of Fame, characterizing the statue The End of the Trail. *For him, Route 66 is a classic transportation corridor best understood by following its origins.*

As a route westward across the U.S., 66 will come down out of Chicago and then make this loop through Oklahoma City and then take off through the West. In the nineteenth century, living in Oklahoma, about where 66 runs now, would depend on geography. West of modern Oklahoma is an open rolling area, and so the native people living there would hunt primarily buffalo, and they were plains-oriented.

By the middle part of the nineteenth century, a lot of the game is gone from the eastern parts of Oklahoma. Moving out onto the Plains, you leave an area where your vistas are relatively enclosed by forest or hills. West of Oklahoma City all of a sudden the land begins to open up and roll, and you have cedars in the draws. The climate begins to change; it gets drier, vegetation is grass.

As you go out there, you get these great vistas. Off in the distance, you would see herds of buffalo several miles away with draws and ravines in between. You're anticipating this great hunt.

I'm always taken in that movie *Dances with Wolves* when they finally come up over that rise, and there's the buffalo herd and everybody goes for them. I always thought if a movie viewer's adrenaline isn't flowing at that time, it's just never flowing. That's what it must have been like, only more so, in reality: "This is it. Here ARE the bison."

To be Kiowa or Cheyenne or Comanche in the 1840s or 1850s in Western Oklahoma was to be at the height of one's power, and life was good. It won't last long. Tragically, the whole way of life will be overwhelmed within a quarter of a century—the coming of the railroads and the Oklahoma land rush.

The buffalo hunters would be a group of thirty to forty people out hunting, sleeping in the evening and camped down along the river bottoms for protection from the wind. When one gets into the Panhandle, into western Oklahoma, wind blows in some direction most of the time. Wood is concentrated along the rivers, and the further west you go, the drier it gets, so having access to water and wood when you camp is where you'd stay.

The people would rise very early and have a meal early and then would be out hunting. You would split up as you traveled out looking for the buffalo herds. Once located, the scouts would come back and say, "We've found them."

The hunters would gather and have an evening meal, and then people would smoke and they would tell stories from the past, talk about the events of the day. Stories are very, very important.

Trappers who'd once traded with Native American people for furs were by the 1850s and '60s trading for buffalo hides. There was a great demand for buffalo hides as carriage blankets and sleigh blankets. In the East, and even in Europe, it became very fashionable. If one wanted to show one's affluence in Central Park in the 1870s on a drive on a cold December day, one snuggled up under a buffalo hide blanket as one went tootling around the park.

Way later, Route 66 injects an awful lot more people into the area who are non-Indians. It will make the travel across the area so much quicker. There's a greater sense of hurry. Once there was a whole rhythm, and a ritual, and the camaraderie of the hunt and the parties going out. These are negated by railroads going west. It's much different—the trek west, the going west—for people who are not Indian. For them, this is an area that has to be crossed and as soon as possible to get someplace where they really want to go. Whereas the crossing of the area itself was for Indian people very much part of the process.

In Oklahoma, tribal people who lived in the region at the time were very much against the railroads going through their land, because they knew that the railroads would transform the nations markedly— because they became avenues of penetration for non-Indian people coming through. So, the railroads become areas where "intruders" will settle. They'll become the death knell of the Indian nations in the period after the Civil War, as they are forced then to open up corridors across their lands for these railroads, and they opposed them very much.

The Five Civilized Tribes wrote petitions to Congress. It was a very legalistic sort of opposition because they realized that armed opposition wasn't going to work. So they argued that this would be an infringement upon their sovereignty.

Later, Indians, like other Oklahomans in the Dust Bowl, took off west along Route 66, toward that golden mecca of economic opportunity that was California. And that's why a lot of Indian people then ended up in the central valley of California, because they, like other Okies, were agricultural workers.

A TOUR ON THE PRAIRIES

WASHINGTON IRVING

– 1832 –

"Route 66 is more than just a span of years and concrete," says Michael Wallis, prominent author of books on the West. "It's what happened there before we connected the dots and put this road together in 1926. That's very, very important—to know it's such an old path, before it was Route 66."

Stagecoaches once rattled along the path of Route 66, wheel spokes glinting in the sun. In the 1830s, before the railroad came, America's most famous writer, Washington Irving, rode from the prairies of eastern Missouri to the Great Plains and back, a thousand miles on horseback. Irving traveled with army rangers and an adventuresome Swiss count (whose recollections follow this chapter). Irving slept in the sweet, balmy air by the river and counted himself lucky to be alive. He found the Osage and other tribes thoughtful and down-to-earth, yet often misunderstood. As he wrote in A Tour on the Prairies, "The Indian of poetical fiction is like the shepherd of pastoral romance, a mere personification of imaginary attributes."

Washington Irving made a career as a satirist after losing interest in a legal career. In The Sketch Book (1819), his adaptations of folktales such as "Rip Van Winkle" and "The Legend of Sleepy Hollow" gave him literary celebrity. He returned to the United States after seventeen years abroad and chronicled the American West in A Tour on the Prairies (1832) and in his Western Journals published posthumously (1944). His verse and biographies made him the most famous American author of the early nineteenth century.

October 12, 1832, in the morning early, the two Creeks who had been sent express by the commander of Fort Gibson, to stop the company of rangers, arrived at our encampment on their return. They had left the company encamped about fifty miles distant, in a fine place on the Arkansas [River], abounding in game, where they intended to await our arrival.

(The Count was well mounted, and, as I have before observed, was a bold and graceful rider. He was fond, too, of caracoling his horse, and dashing about in the buoyancy of youthful spirits . . .) It was a bright sunny morning, with a pure transparent atmosphere that seemed to bathe the very heart with gladness. Our march continued parallel to the Arkansas, through a rich and varied country; sometimes we had to break our way through alluvial bottoms matted with redundant vegetation, where the gigantic trees were entangled with grape-vines, hanging like cordage from their branches; sometimes we coasted along sluggish brooks, whose feebly trickling current just served to link to-gether a succession of glassy ponds, imbedded like mirrors in the quiet bosom of the forest, reflecting its autumnal foliage, and patches of the clear blue sky. Sometimes we scrambled up broken and rocky hills, from the summits of which we had wide views stretching on one side over distant prairies diversified by groves and forests, and on the other ranging along a line of blue and shadowy hills beyond the waters of the Arkansas . . .

In crossing a prairie of moderate extent rendered little better than a slippery bog by the recent showers, we were overtaken by a violent thunder-gust. The rain came rattling upon us in torrents, and spat-tered up like steam along the ground; the whole landscape was sud-denly wrapped in gloom that gave a vivid effect to the intense sheets of lightning, while the thunder seemed to burst over our very heads, and was reverberated by the groves and forests that checkered and skirted the prairie. Man and beast were so pelted, drenched, and confounded, that the line was thrown in complete confusion.

A thunder-storm on a prairie, as upon the ocean, derives grandeur and sublimity from the wild and boundless waste over which it rages and bellows.

After a toilsome march of some distance through a country cut up by ravines and brooks, and entangled by thickets, we emerged upon a grand prairie. Here one of the characteristic scenes of the Far West broke upon us. An immense extent of grassy, undulating, or, as it is termed, rolling country, with here and there a clump of trees, dimly seen in the distance like a ship at sea; the landscape deriving sublimity from its vastness and simplicity. To the southwest, on the summit of a hill, was a singular crest of broken rocks, resembling a ruined fortress. The weather was verging into that serene but somewhat arid season called the Indian Summer. There was a smoky haze in the atmosphere that tempered the brightness of the sunshine into a golden tint, softening the features of the landscape, and giving a vagueness to the outlines of distant objects. This haziness was daily increasing, and was attributed to the burning of distant prairies by the Indian hunting parties.

We had not gone far upon the prairie before we came to where deeply-worn footpaths were seen traveling the country: sometimes two or three would keep on parallel to each other, and but a few paces apart. These were pronounced to be traces of buffaloes, where large droves had passed. There were also tracks of horses.

ON THE WESTERN TOUR WITH WASHINGTON IRVING

COUNT DE POURTALÈS

– 1832 –

Under the sway of the French Romantic philosopher and author Jean-Jacques Rousseau was Irving's companion, the Count Albert-Alexandre de Portalès, "a bold and graceful rider." For the count, as for Wordsworth, "the Earth is apparel'd in a celestial light." He is swept away by the grandeur of his situation, writing in a style that today some would find flowery: "There is something grandiose about these plains which, as far as the eye can see, are thickly covered with grass varied in color and watered by little streams . . . The gold of the flowers is offset by the violet of the thistle." He was equally ingenuous about the Indians he and Irving met.

The French sold their claim to this region in 1803, yet the metaphoric power of this vast swath of country—larger than France itself—proved irresistible to the imagination of writers like Chateaubriand, who had placed monkeys on the riverbanks of the Mississippi in his novellas Atala *and* René. *A similar exoticism colors the Count de Pourtalès's account, as he evokes what it was like to travel this corridor before railroads and highways pushed through. The count's closing comment about using camels for transport would, as we shall see, prove prophetic for travel along the thirty-fifth parallel.*

October 9, 1832: Tomorrow morning we leave with a detachment of riders to join the Indians on their buffalo hunt. They will push on to the Red River, a tributary of the Mississippi marking the border between the United States and Mexico. Here we are then condemned to spend a month with nothing over our heads but a tent or an Indian hut—but it is with great pleasure that I submit to these hardships . . .

Osage horsemen, with whom we are going hunting, are really the best people in the world. They are hospitable, generous and love the whites with all their hearts. I have eagerly begun to learn their language. I am assured that I shall be able to understand it and even speak it within two weeks. . . . You can see that we do not even face enough danger to make this expedition romantic. The climate itself conspires against my taste for adventure. The weather is magnificent. All the rattlesnakes, copperheads, centipedes, and mosquitoes are in their winter quarters. For five months now I have been traveling through the woods, the fields, and the prairies of the New World and I have yet to see a poisonous reptile, dead or alive. You can see how baseless your European fears are. Besides, since I am dressed from head to toe in a double thickness of deerskin, I could roll on twenty snakes without danger. My costume is a strange mixture of Indian and European. I am wearing a leather shirt, leggings, and moccasins, which I find much more comfortable than shoes when I am on horseback. I do not know how I shall become re-accustomed to civilization. I have given up ties, knives, forks, bed sheets, mattresses, and all the superfluous things which, as Jean-Jacques [Rousseau] says, turn man into a dull brute. . . . We never drink anything but water. Sometimes it is heated by the sun or muddied by our horses' hooves, but our thirst makes it taste delicious. Our food is good. We have deer, prairie-hen, wild turkey, squirrel, and grilled, boiled, raw, cooked, and fried corn. We pick wild grapes in groves of trees in the middle of the prairies. We have coffee and sassafras tea. Everything is seasoned with a hellish appetite, our good humor, and the long and original tales of the French Creole hunters . . .

October 10: At noon we were joined by W. Irving and a company of Rangers. They are to take us to the rest of the group, which went on ahead two or three days ago. Several miles from Canadian Fork we passed a long line of wooden huts inhabited by Creeks. The fertility of their land and the surrounding territory is astonishing, even though they have not yet attained the agricultural level of the other Americans . . .

October 19: We left about eight o'clock as usual and began a difficult trek through the woods, which ran along the edge of the prairie. Some of the men who preferred going across the prairie rather than through the woods felt that they were justified in thinking that we were needlessly circling the prairie. Some of the others, including the captain, tried to argue the point. After half an hour, we came back to our starting place. A little while later, the sky, which for several days had been covered with a strange mixture of smoke and clouds, seemed to open, as a torrential rain began to fall. Because of the excessive heat we were able to tell for two days that a storm was on its way. Lightning flashed, thunder rolled, and the sky was full of fire and water. Lightning struck a short distance from us and routed from its shelter a herd of deer, which bounded off and disappeared into the woods. In a few moments our deerskin coats and jackets and my two shirts were soaked through. Shivering and ranting in the water that dripped from everything, at long last we found a delightful campsite. It was an English garden, except for the fact that the grass was taller and that it was burnt by the summer heat. After some time and effort, we succeeded in lighting a fire and we pitched our tent. Our men quickly stretched out some skins with which to build a shelter and formed a type of cradle with tree branches. Dry clothing followed by a good supper of fritters, moose, deer, and bear finally restored us.

October 21: It has just occurred to me that the introduction of the dromedary to this country would be of inestimable value. This animal could be used to carry on trade with Santa Fe and the interior of Mexico. I do not doubt that the use of this animal will become widespread. What great help it would be in crossing the terrible pampas of Peru . . .

If I ever settle in America, it will be in this area, the only place in the United States which offers a romantic way of life plus absolute independence. I would surround myself with a double rampart of Osages to protect me against the Americans, those commercial Thebans of the New World.

THE JOURNALS OF THE SUPERINTENDENT OF THE WAGON WORLD

EDWARD F. BEALE

– 1858 –

In the summer and winter of 1857, Lieutenant Edward F. Beale made an epic journey to survey a wagon road west along the thirty-fifth parallel, the future route of Route 66, from Albuquerque to the Colorado River. Beale famously took up the suggestion of Jefferson Davis to use camels imported from Africa as pack animals. As the following excerpt shows, if he was in love with the wild, dry country separating the high plains of New Mexico, the mountains of Arizona, and the lush Colorado River, he was even more inflamed by the success of his camel train. Following in the footsteps of Whipple and other explorers, Beale's team arrived at the Colorado River on January 1, 1858. He had canvassed the resources of wood, water, game, and human settlements along this great distance. After him came a wagon road, stagecoaches, railroads, and then, of course, Route 66 and a car-traveling nation. The California that had come to fame through the tales of Mark Twain and the legends of the forty-niners was now becoming an overland destination. As Dave Edmunds pointed out in a previous selection, this meant a vast intrusion of American settlers into regions once dominated by Spanish-Mexicans and Indians. Out of this vast mezcla of traveler and rancher, native and foreigner, came the dynamic mix that is the American Southwest today.

As a young navy lieutenant, Edward Fitzgerald Beale made six trips across the country from ocean to ocean. After he brought news of the discovery of gold to Washington, and a bag of the stuff, he was a logical choice for wagon-road superintendent.

Sir: I have the honor to transmit herewith my daily journal of the survey made last summer and winter of a wagon road from Fort Defiance to the Colorado River or State line of California, near the thirty-fifth parallel. With this journal I send also an itinerary from Albuquerque, in New Mexico, to California. This itinerary gives distances as they exist, no air lines or imaginary curves, but every turn of our wheels recorded by the odometer attached . . .

The journal which I send you is a faithful history of each day's work, written at the camp fire at the close of every day. I have not altered or changed it in any respect whatever, as I desired to speak of the country as it impressed me on the spot, so as to be as faithful in my description of it as possible. You will therefore find it very rough, but I hope those who may follow in my footsteps over the road may find it correct in every particular. I have written it for the use of emigrants more than for show. If it answers the purpose of assisting them I shall be well satisfied.

I presume there can be no further question as to the practicability of the country near the thirty-fifth parallel for a wagon road, since Aubrey, Whipple, and myself, have all traveled it successfully with wagons, neither of us in precisely the same line, and yet through very much the same country . . .

The rain has brought the grass forward wonderfully, and with it an abundance of beautiful flowers, so that the prairie for the last few days has been filled with perfume and richly colored flowers, which would have been no disgrace to the most costly hothouse. The whole of the country is vastly improved by these grateful showers, which have clothed it everywhere with verdure, and filled the air with fragrance.

Of large game we have seen but little, but turkeys and partridges abound in great numbers; in fact, the whistle of "Bob White" is with us all the time.

The camels came into camp with us. We find one great trouble, and the only one, in managing them, is that we know nothing about the method of packing them, and have it all to learn. It seems that they like most the herbs and boughs of bitter bushes, which all other animals reject. The more I see of them the more interested in them I become, and the more I am convinced of their usefulness. Their perfect docility and patience under difficulties renders them invaluable, and my only regret at present is that I have not double the number.

I rode on to camp again alone, and arrived after an absence of three hours, during which I had ridden twenty-seven miles. "Seid," the white dromedary, seemed not the least tired; indeed, it was as much as I could do to hold him on my return, and could not have done so had I not put the chain part of his halter around his lower jaw. The best mule or horse in our camp, in present condition, could not have performed the same journey in twice the time, although they have been fed with corn ever since leaving, and some of the horses not worked at all, having been kept for express duty in the event of an accident, while "Seid" has not only worked every day, but been grazed entirely on grass.

I saw some Indians, in the hills at a distance, as I rode along.

I found our men had been fishing again and had caught, at one haul of our gunny bag net, ninety-six fine fish, which furnished us a good meal for all hands . . .

Fancy a great mountain range running in an unbroken line for miles and miles, and here rent asunder, so that a road perfectly level passes directly through what would otherwise present an impassable barrier, and the rock rising in a solid mass, five hundred feet perpendicular, on each side.

This cleft is about a hundred yards in width and about three miles in length. . . . Our walk this morning was constantly through the grandest scenery, and fully repaid us for rising so early.

August 27: This morning, everything being in readiness, we take leave of our kind and hospitable friends and start upon our journey into the wilderness. No one who has not commanded an expedition of this kind, where everything ahead is dim, uncertain, and unknown, except the dangers, can imagine the anxiety with which I start upon this journey. Not only responsible for the lives of my men, but my reputation and the highest wrought expectations of my friends, and the still more highly wrought expectations of envious enemies—all these dependent on the next sixty days' good or evil fortune . . .

My admiration for the camels increases daily with my experience of them. The harder the test they are put to the more fully they seem to justify all that can be said of them. They pack water for others four days under a hot sun and never get a drop; they pack heavy burdens of corn and oats for months and never get a grain; and on the bitter greasewood and other worthless shrubs not only subsist but keep fat;

withal, they are so perfectly docile and so admirably contented with whatever fate befalls them. No one could do justice to their merits or value in expeditions of this kind, and I look forward to the day when every mail route across the continent will be conducted and worked altogether with this economical and noble brute.

RAILROADERS' ROUTE 66

MICHAEL AMUNDSON

– 1890s –

Beale's expedition proved the possibility of a land route to California across the Mountain West along the thirty-fifth parallel. Railroads arrived soon after, following Senator Thomas Hart Benton's vision of railroads "from sea to shining sea." There are places today, such as Winslow, Arizona, where Beale's road to California can be seen on the ground, in wagon wheel ruts only a hundred feet from the railroad tracks. Route 66 passes ten feet away from these same ruts. This transportation corridor was set in place, finally, by the coming of the twenty or so railroad companies that graded the roadbed for the later highway. Later, Route 66 would take up its grade, stops, and eventually its passengers.

Professor Amundson reminds us that the railroads brought not only the physical infrastructure for building Route 66, but they also set in motion a cultural dynamic between visitors and natives, particularly in the Southwest.

Michael Amundson writes about mining and the nuclear West and teaches at Northern Arizona University. His books include Wyoming: Time and Time Again *(1991),* Yellowcake Towns: Uranium Mining in the American West *(2002), and* Passage to Wonderland: Re-photographing Joseph Stimson's Scenes from Cody to Yellowstone National Park, 1903 and 2008 *(forthcoming).*

The connection between the railroad and Route 66 is essential in understanding either one of them—especially for understanding Route 66, because the migration across the Southwest to California is embedded first by wagon roads, following old Indian trails, and then the railroads and the telegraph.

The whole communication and transportation infrastructure of the Southwest is organized in an east-west fashion, and it follows out of New Mexico and into California along Beale's Road. You have the Atlantic and Pacific Railroad in 1881–1882, cutting across New Mexico and Texas, across the thirty-fifth parallel, through Flagstaff and then on to California.

By the 1890s, the most important transition in this western movement is Fred Harvey and the Harvey Company. Fred Harvey got his start in restaurants and then got a contract in what became the Atchison, Topeka and Santa Fe Railroad, to operate eateries along the railroad. Eventually the Harvey House became synonymous with good service.

At the same time the Harvey Company is important because they began to create the "Southwest"—that is, they created what they believed was an image that Americans wanted (and marketed it). This is happening at the same time industrialization is taking place in the eastern United States. People wanted a simpler life—arts and crafts, handmade items were very popular—and people traveling on the railroad, going through the Southwest, start to stop at these Harvey Houses, and the Harvey Company set up museums in their spots.

I am talking about the past, but when we go back and look at Route 66, the theme in variation becomes apparent. The Harvey Company would set up a museum of Hopi Kachina dolls at their gift shops. They even would go so far as to go to traders like Lorenzo Hubble at Ganado, Arizona, and say, "The red blankets sell better than the blue blankets—tell the Navajo to make red blankets." And so they started to shape what people started to see.

The railroads commodified Native Americans. It gave Native Americans opportunity in a society that really gave them very few opportunities: you can make goods for us to sell to tourists. Route 66 did the same thing. It enabled people, it gave them opportunities.

Around 1915, as automobiles are becoming more popular, and more roads are feasible, the Harvey Company picks up on what they call the Indian Detours. Women were the guides, "detourists." They would drive automobiles from jumping-off points at the Harvey Hotels in places later on Route 66 like Gallup, New Mexico, or Winslow, Arizona, or Albuquerque or Santa Fe. Then the Harvey Company pretty much dies out, and the Indian Detours fail with the Great Depression.

Henry Ford, with the Model T, has created a car for the masses, and now you have this whole new mode of transportation. But people still want to go to the same places and see the same things, and so it's not surprising that what's created around Route 66 is following the same lines of what has already been created before.

Take Flagstaff, Arizona. By the 1930s and 1940s, people realized that you don't have to be centrally located. Flagstaff reinvents itself as a Route 66 town. Instead of people traveling along the railroad, which they were still doing, they were more and more traveling along the highway, along Route 66.

People realized that they could expand further and further away from the downtown core of the town to give them a better advantage along the route. So Flagstaff elongates along Route 66. The railroad is right next to it, but it never spread out like that because the railroad controlled where people exited. But now that Route 66 is here as they drive into town, someone builds on the furthest edge of town and they build a motel and somebody builds next to them.

ONE NIGHT IN THE RED DOG SALOON

HAL G. EVARTS, JR.

– 1840s –

After Lieutenant Beale had traced a line from New Mexico to California, many of the camels in his expedition were released—or escaped on their own—to wander the dusty ridges between California and Arizona. Pretty soon these camels turned from legendary figures into mythical ones, and camel sightings occurred across the desert Southwest.

Camels were seen within the memory of the cowboy era of the West, in the nineteenth century, and Hal Evarts has fashioned a story of a rogue in the western tall-tale tradition of Pecos Bill or Sam Bass. When Jefferson Davis, as secretary of the interior, wanted to use camels to explore the West, or to deliver the mail, he had no idea what he'd started—not just in the Civil War, but in securing notoriety for the path that railroads and the Mother Road would eventually take.

Writing in the 1950s, Evarts incorporated the prejudices of his time, asserting an us-against-them attitude in Indian-white relations. Hal Evarts's career as a writer of films and TV series extended from the silent picture era to the 1960s. His series of westerns that began in the 1920s, including The Yellow Horde *and* Fur Brigade: Trappers of the Early West, *followed in the footsteps of Zane Grey and others, helping to create the genre. This story is an adaptation of an old folktale type ("Amazing Animal Encounters"), a cousin to yarns about mermaids and unicorns. His hero's name, Lew Zane, is an obvious homage to that great author of the Old West, Zane Grey.*

It started one afternoon last fall when Lew rode into Red Dog and tied up out front. Soon as word spread, the boys smiled to themselves and got ready. Merchants put up their window shutters, the bartenders took down their mirrors and fancy glasses. Just in case. Lew hadn't hardly more than got settled in the Golden Nugget here when Long Jim Lannigan ambled up to his table.

Maybe Long Jim ain't the best sheriff we ever had but he's a stickler for the law. A tall lanky party, he's as big and tough as Lew and almost as close-mouthed . . .

"How's about letting me keep your guns tonight?"

"I don't reckon, Sheriff," Lew said. "Might want to shoot out some windows later." That seemed reasonable but, like I say, this Lew is a very honest, peace-loving citizen. He pulled a buckskin bag out of his pocket and dumped a trickle of gold dust on the table.

"Like to pay in advance," he said. "For the windows, I mean."

Long Jim gave him a sorrowful look and shook his head, then walked out. The sheriff's attitude hurt Lew. It was a point of honor with him to pay his debts. Always did. He just couldn't understand that reproachful look of Long Jim's. Got to brooding so it sort of spoiled his fun. So he wasn't rightly himself when a pair of sharpers drifted over to the table and suggested a game of penny ante. They'd seen that poke of gold dust too.

Well sir, one thing led to another, and pretty soon Lew had cleaned out every gambler in the house, not caring a hoot. The more he drank the soberer he got, the wilder he bet the more he won, until chips were stacked up chin-high in front of him. Then Acey-Ducey Dugan dealt himself into the game.

Acey-Ducey Dugan was real artistic with a deck of cards. He owned two saloons, a pearl stickpin, the flashiest diamond ring in town, and he couldn't abide lucky amateurs like Lew. When he took a hand we looked for action. First off he lost his cash, next his stickpin, then his ring, and when the next big pot came up he tossed in his deed to the Golden Nugget . . .

Near sunrise Lew climbed on up the ridge but his horse started acting skittish. He gave her a cuff and all of a sudden a big black shape reared off the ground and let out a bellow. The horse jumped straight up in the air and Lew, all loose in the saddle, went sailing off and cracked his head on a rock.

When he woke up, the sun was beating down in his face and his head was pounding like a tom-tom. He felt the lump behind his ear, then felt in his coat for the bottle, which somehow had been spared. Grateful for that, Lew took a snort and sat up to look for his horse. Instead he saw a big, brown, shaggy critter watching him with mournful eyes not ten yards away. Too big for a bear and too rank-smelling for a cow. Besides, it had a green beard and a humped back.

Lew shut his eyes tight, spit out his mouthful of whiskey, and flopped back on the rock. When a man got to seeing camels in the middle of the desert it was time to quit. Past time, 'way past. John Barleycorn was panting down his neck. Lew lay there shivering and sweating but by and by he noticed a strange thing: that animal stink was as strong as ever. Cautious-like he opened one eye a crack and sure enough that camel was still a-staring at him.

A weaker man might've cracked right there, but not Lew Zane. He got up shaky on his feet and circled round the beast. It was real, a genuine one-hump camel, hunkered down on its knees. An old male, he guessed, gaunted in the ribs and flank and ugly as sin. All the teeth was gone and saliva had dribbled down its chin like a moss goatee, but them big, soft eyes had the most piteous look Lew had ever seen, almost human. Someways that look reminded him of Long Jim Lannigan. Finally Lew stepped in close and put a hand on its neck. The camel rolled over on one side and whimpered like a sick dog. Then he saw what the trouble was. A prickly-pear cactus had stuck in the left hind footpad like a pincushion and the leg was beginning to swell. The poor old brute couldn't walk.

Lew felt relieved to learn he didn't have the fantods after all, but he was mighty puzzled. How come a camel to be way out here? Near as he could recollect camels belonged in Africa, a far piece from Arizona Territory. Runaway from a circus, he thought, but that was silly . . .

The camel had settled back on its haunches, looking all forlorn. Lew couldn't bear to shoot it now. "You mangy old buzzard bait," he said. "No wonder them horses lit out when they got a whiff of you."

Then he noticed a kind of scar on one hip. It was furred over, but he squatted down close and saw the brand USA had been burned into the hide. He got to remembering his grandpappy who'd been a soldier on the frontier way back in the fifties, before the war. His grandpappy had seen camels, some of the bunch Jeff Davis had shipped over for the

War Department to haul mail out west. Lew scratched his head, trying to recollect the story.

Seemed like the experiment hadn't worked. The camels scared the cavalry mounts, the soldiers hated the camels, and the Army cussed Jeff Davis proper. So they sold 'em off and turned 'em loose. And the camels disappeared. This one, Lew allowed, must've been wandering around on his lonesome for close to thirty years. Didn't seem possible, but there was a U.S. Army brand to prove it.

"You done me a favor, Moss Face," Lew said. "Looks like I got to doctor you up."

So he got out his knife and started on that cactus. It was a messy job prying the stuff loose, and Lew got all stuck up himself, but the camel never let out a bleat, though the spines had worked in deep. Gamest thing he ever did see. But he'd doctored enough horses to know there was still a danger of infection. What he needed was a disinfectant. That's when Lew Zane showed he'd got a heart as big as all creation. Quite a tussle with his conscience but he done it. Picked up his bottle, near half a quart left, pulled out the cork with his teeth, and poured it all on Hump Back's punctured foot. Old Hump blubbered a little but took it like a soldier, like a real old army trooper. Made Lew feel right proud.

The camel lumbered to his feet this time and limped down to the spring. Lew drank, too, but the water tasted flat. Gave the beast a friendly slap on the rump and set off to shag his horse. Hadn't gone a hundred yards before the camel hobbled up behind him. "Look," Lew said, "you're in no shape to travel, and I got me a horse to catch."

He went on a little ways and old Moss Face limped right after him. Kinda exasperated, Lew stopped again. "We're even, ain't we? Go on back to water, Git!"

He shied a rock, but the camel didn't move, just watched him with those weepy eyes . . .

'Long about dinnertime he was passing a big rock when Long Jim Lannigan stepped out with a rifle. Behind him stood two horses, one of which was Lew's.

"Hoddy, Sheriff," Lew said.

"Hoddy, Lew," Long Jim said.

Lew hoped maybe everything was going to be all right now that Long Jim had caught his horse, and he said, "I'm sorry about Acey-Ducey Dugan."

"What for?"

"Well," Lew said, "he ran a nice, quiet saloon."

"That he did," Long Jim said. "But Acey-Ducey ain't what's botherin' me, Lew. It's the way you sneaked off without payin' for them windows you busted."

Lew could tell the sheriff was riled, the way he kept pointing that Winchester. "Why, plumb slipped my mind, but I'll pay you right now," he said, and shoved a hand in his pocket.

Catch was, he didn't have a nickel. He'd left his money and dust poke on the table in the Golden Nugget the night before. Feeling sheepish, he said, "Reckon you'll have to trust me, Sheriff, till I dig some more dust back in the hills."

Long Jim shook his head. "Hate to say this, Lew, but you own the Golden Nugget now. Never did trust a saloon keeper."

Lew's face went pale. He knew Long Jim didn't hold with drinking but he'd clean forgot that handsome straight club flush. Just couldn't believe he'd won the Golden Nugget. Great roarin' Jupiter! His own saloon! "Can't you trust me till we get to town?" he said.

"Have to," Long Jim wrinkled his nose. "What's that smell on you? Skunk?

Lew sniffed at his shirt. "Camel," he said. "Darndest thing happened to me—"

THE U.P. TRAIL

ZANE GREY

– 1870s –

Those heading west along Indian trails faced challenges scarcely imaginable. Beale's camels might have crossed streams and rocky canyons with relative ease, but a chain of steel and wheels could not.

In The U.P. Trail, Zane Grey caught the spirit of Americans at work. This was a people prepared to triumph over every obstacle, physical or economic: high drama written in iron rails and wooden plank. Connecting the different parts of a great land was a glory, involving the building of trestles, bridges, roadbed, and intersections for the first intercontinental railroads and highways.

If there is a throbbing quality about Grey's prose, if he makes the building of railroads comparable to the building of the Pyramids, he writes in the tradition of Walt Whitman's stories of the Civil War and Jack London's of Alaska—a respect for honest work and for those who do it year after year. "Progress was great," Grey writes. Without it, "there would be no transportation save horse, mule, and human." Only the old trapper at the end of this selection understands how Progress has its cost: the greed of railroad owners taking a dark toll.

Grey wrote over ninety books, many of them best sellers, in a lustrous career spanning more than a half-century. He saw both sides in the equation of developing the West: the grandeur of human ambition and the despoliation of virgin land. The old prospector's lament at the end of this selection suggests Grey's own stance.

The wonderful idea of uniting East and West by a railroad originated in one man's brain; he lived for it, and finally he died for it. But the seeds he had sown were fruitful. One by one other men divined and believed, despite doubt and fear, until the day arrived when Congress put the Government of the United States, the army, a group of frock-coated directors, and unlimited gold back of General Lodge, and bade him build the road . . .

General Lodge himself explained the difficulties of the situation and what the young surveyor was expected to do. Neale flushed with pride; his eyes flashed; his jaw set. But he said little while the engineers led him out to the scene of the latest barrier. It was a rugged gorge, old and yellow and crumbled, cedar-fringed at the top, bare and white at the bottom. The approach to it was through a break in the walls, so that the gorge really extended both above and below this vantage-point.

"This is the only pass through these foot-hills," said Engineer Henney, the eldest of Lodge's corps.

The passage ended where the break in the walls fronted abruptly upon the gorge. It was a wild scene. Only inspired and dauntless men could have entertained any hope of building a railroad through such a place. The mouth of the break was narrow; a rugged slope led up to the left; to the right a huge buttress of stone wall bulged over the gorge; across stood the seamed and cracked cliffs, and below yawned the abyss. The nearer side of the gorge could only be guessed at.

Neale crawled to the extreme edge of the precipices, and, lying flat, he tried to discover what lay beneath. Evidently he did not see much, for upon getting up, he shook his head. Then he gazed at the bulging wall.

"The side of that can be blown off," he muttered.

"But what's around the corner? If it's straight stone wall for miles and miles we are done," said Boone, another of the engineers . . .

"It only looks bad," he said. "We'll climb to the top and I'll go down over the wall on a rope."

Neale had been let down over many precipices in those stony hills. He had been the luckiest, the most daring and successful of all the men picked out and put to perilous tasks. No one spoke of the accidents that had happened, or even the fatal fall of a lineman who a few weeks before had ventured once too often. Every rod of road surveyed made the engineers sterner at their task, just as it made them keener to attain final success.

The climb to the top of the bluff was long and arduous. The whole corps went, and also some of the troopers.

"I'll need a long rope," Neale had said to King, his lineman . . .

"There's a bulge of rock. I can't see what's below it," he said. "No use for signals. I'll go down the length of the rope and trust to find a footing. I can't be hauled up."

They all conceded this silently.

Then Neale sat down, let his legs dangle over the wall, firmly grasped his instrument, and said to the troopers who held the rope, "All right!"

They lowered him foot by foot.

It was windy and the dust blew up from under the wall. Black canyon swifts, like swallows, darted out with rustling wings, uttering frightened twitterings. The engineers leaned over, watching Neale's progress. Larry King did not look over the precipice. He watched the slowly slipping rope as knot by knot it passed over. It fascinated him.

The gorge lay asleep in the westering sun, silent, full of blue haze. Seen from this height, far above the break where the engineers had first halted, it had the dignity and dimensions of a canyon. Its walls had begun to change color in the sunset light.

"He's reached the bulge of rock," called Baxter, craning his neck.

"There, he's down—out of sight!" exclaimed Henney.

Casey, the flagman, leaned farther out than any other. "Phwat a dom' sthrange way to build a railroad, I sez," he remarked . . .

[Neale saw the thousands of plodding, swearing, fighting, blaspheming, joking laborers on the field of action—saw the picture they made, red and bronzed and black, dust-begrimed; and how here with the ties and the rails and the road-bed was the heart of that epical turmoil. What approach could great and rich engineers and directors have made to that vast enterprise without these sons of brawn? Neale now saw what he had once dreamed, and that was the secret of his longing to get down to the earth with these men.

One day he drove spikes for hours, with the gangs in uninterrupted labor around him, while back a mile along the road the troopers fought the Sioux; and all this time, when any moment he might be ordered to drop his sledge for a rifle, he listened to the voices in his memory and saw the faces.

Another day dawned in which he saw the grading gangs return from work ahead. They were done. Streams of horses, wagons, and men on the return! They had met the graders from the west, and the two lines of road-bed had been connected. As these gangs passed, cheer on cheer greeted them from the rail-layers. It was a splendid moment . . .]

The old trapper was glad to see the last of habitations, and of men, and of the railroad. Slingerland hated that great, shining steel band of progress connecting East and West. Every ringing sledge-hammer blow had sung out the death-knell of the trapper's calling. This railroad spelled the end of the wilderness. What one group of greedy men had accomplished others would imitate; and the grass of the plains would be burned, the forests blackened, the fountains dried up in the valleys, and the wild creatures of the mountains driven and hunted and exterminated. The end of the buffalo had come—the end of the Indian was in sight—and that of the fur-bearing animal and his hunter must follow soon with the hurrying years.

Slingerland hated the railroad, and he could not see as Neale did, or any of the engineers or builders. This old trapper had the vision of the Indian—that far-seeing eye cleared by distance and silence, and the force of the great, lonely hills. Progress was great, but nature undespoiled was greater. If a race could not breed all stronger men, through its great movements, it might better not breed any, for the bad over-multiplied the good, and so their needs magnified into greed. Slingerland saw many shining bands of steel across the plains and mountains, many stations and hamlets and cities, a growing and marvelous prosperity from timber, mines, farms, and in the distant end—a gutted West.

RECALLING ROUTE 66'S
TRAIL OF TEARS

MAN SUSANYATAME

– 1880s –

It wasn't only the old prospectors and trappers who watched with regret as the ranchers and then the railroads cut a trail across the open range of the West. The railroads and Route 66 would cross dozens of Indian nations along their path.

One of these was the Hualapai, cousins to the many Pai peoples of the American Southwest. Today, the Hualapai occupy about a million acres in their Peach Springs reservation, about one-sixth of their ancestral lands.

The loss of these lands preoccupies those elders who remember it, including unofficial tribal historian Man Susanyatame. Few accounts exist of Route 66's own Trail of Tears, where the Hualapai were marched along a path Route 66 would follow when Mohave County ranchers declared their land vacant and then sold a right-of-way to the railroad builders. With the loss of land and lack of water holes came the decimation of custom and language seen across Indian country in the West.

The Hualapai once ranged freely across the western edge of the Grand Canyon. Fifty years after the coming of the railroad and road builders, they became scouts, laborers, and car mechanics, as Route 66 passed north. Today the tribe lives mainly on tourism: Route 66 visitors, backpackers, and river-rafting tours.

Ronald "Man" Susanyatame traveled Route 66 to elementary school and for the rest of his life. He worked at the Grand Canyon Caverns, a prominent Route 66 landmark.

My name is Ronald Susanyatame. Around here, they just call me Man. I was born here on the reservation, up here about seven miles. A place we call Blue Mountain, but in Indian we call it Winyah. I was born there with the Pine Spring Band, which encompasses territories clear to Colorado. When 66 was through here we had five gas stations that were running twenty-four hours a day, some of them.

Our older Hualapai are just passing on. We need to establish some program where the kids want to learn. In time they'll see what they're missing out, and hopefully come back and learn those things. Tanning deer hide—nobody does that around here anymore. I do. And weaving sandals out of yucca.

We stress to them: you got to do it now. Because when we're going, my age group, then who's going to teach you? Who's going to say this is right, this is wrong? There was an old Hualapai holy man. He knew long before anybody that there was going to be a race of people that are going to move in, pale skins. "They're going to take your land, your culture, your soul, if you let them, everything." But these big traditional territories that we had, we didn't protect it.

Anyway, the ranchers moved in. They started taking the springs. We tried to hang on, but it was too much. And of course the disease that they brought with them killed a lot of us. And then the final blow was they sent us to La Paz. That's about two hundred miles, down below Parker.

The U.S. Army took them all down there in 1875. They marched them to Kingman and then to Oatman, along what would be 66, on the west side of Kingman. That's the place we call Hucklemoya. They had a fort there. Then they corralled them all up in a square-mile area. And then from there, they made them walk all they way down there.

By '76, the Hualapai couldn't take it anymore, because we're mountain people. So they just said, "We might as well die trying to get back," so they all escaped that area. They came back here thinking that the water, everything, was still going to be here. But when they got back, they were all taken up. The springs—especially the big springs. The good hunting areas. Everything was . . . you know. After that, they went to work for ranchers, the railroad, in town, mines, just doing what they can.

The old 66 comes from Kingman, down towards Yucca. And then it turns up, goes into Oatman, and there's areas in there where Hualapai lived. In the old days, Okies came knocking at the door—everything that they owned on that one little car, plus the people in it. They'd stop by the house, and my grandmother couldn't talk English. At first she was scared, but then she realized the predicament they were in, a whole bunch of kids, so she'd give them something to do, plus give them food. My uncle, he was mechanically inclined. If their car was broken down, well, get that old reliable baling wire, fix everything up for them and send them on their way. But when I-40 came bypassing 66, then everything just slowed down to a crawl.

The interaction, I think it's all the same. We're still trying to understand them; they're still trying to understand us. In 1950-something, I worked at the Grand Canyon Caverns on 66, building the sidewalks down there. Going down, they have an elevator, but before, they just had a ladder and you couldn't see that well without lights. But then they got electricity down in there. God, it's dark in there. It gets all pitch black and you hear a lot of things.

In Hualapai [mythology] there is always a keeper of that area. He can help you, he can hurt you, he can scare you. If you're thinking good thoughts, everything will work out good. But if you're not yourself, then things happen. Out here on the reservation, we still make little houses for little people, guardians of that canyon. Leave them food, water.

Today, there's a lot of destruction that we don't like, but we can't do anything. These people, they own the land, they have a piece of paper that says they own the land, and they can do anything they want with it. The elders, they cry when they go by, "Why are they doing this? Why isn't anybody stopping them?" And we tell them, we can't. What I would like to see, when there's something on the reservation, nobody's taking it and putting it someplace else. (Unless you go through a blessing, that's the only time you can take things.) And they're taking these big huge boulders, loading them in trucks, and putting them in front of buildings, office buildings. I don't know why. Like they didn't have any rocks in their area, or they just want mine.

Peach Springs

SPRING MTS. (11,918 FT.)
WHITE HILLS
DETRITAL VALLEY
ARIZONA
95
93
NEW YORK MTS.
CHLORIDE
L. MOHAVE
SEARCHLIGHT JCT.
GOLDROAD
ED'S CAMP
GOFFS
OATMAN
66
FENNER
SOUTH PASS
FT. MOHAVE
NEEDLES
GOLDEN SHORES
OLD WOMAN MTS.
TOPOCK
CHEMEHUEVI RANGE
CHEMEHUEVI VAL.
HAVASU
L.H. CITY
DANBY LAKE
LAKE HAVASU
IRON MTS.
WHIPPLE MTS.

A BIOREGIONAL APPROACH
TO ROUTE 66:

AN INTRODUCTION

In the sections that follow, Route 66 is examined from a bioregional viewpoint. Route 66 cuts across the major bioregions of the North American continent. The glaciated outwash and moraine country of the Midwest, with its licorice-colored, fertile valleys: Prairie 66. The vast, blowing, wide-open spaces of the Great Plains, beginning in Oklahoma and stretching through to the Llano Estacado of New Mexico: Plains 66. The high ridges and plateaus of Central and Western New Mexico, over the Continental Divide, and across Arizona to the Colorado River: Mountain 66. The vast Mojave Desert, high plains, and San Gabriel Valley leading to the Los Angeles basin: Desert 66. And then the lush California coast, where Route 66 ends (or begins): Coastal 66.

The next sections are divided according to these regions, grouped by states: Illinois, Missouri, and Kansas; Oklahoma and Texas; New Mexico and Arizona; and California, whose diverse geography encompasses many of these bioregions. Essays in each of these sections cover most of the twentieth century, from the teens to the '60s.

PRAIRIE 66

ILLINOIS, MISSOURI, AND KANSAS

Where U.S. Route 66 began—
Michigan Ave. at Jackson Blvd., Chicago
(3 A.M., Tuesday, September 27, 1988)

THE SANTA FE TRAIL

VACHEL LINDSAY

– 1914 –

----

*Beginning this bioregional approach is Vachel Lindsay, one of the Mid-
west's great poets. The Midwest is not a region one thinks of first when
"Route 66" is spoken aloud. Its gentle valleys lack the drama of the open
spaces of the plains or the rugged majesty of the high piney woods farther
west. Yet Illinois's Route 66 was the first stretch of the road to be paved. In
its path, leaving Chicago and the Great Lakes and heading to the Great
River, we find traces of old Indian migratory trails.*

*Lindsay writes a decade before planning for Route 66 began, in the
heyday of the Good Roads Movement, when highway planners were knit-
ting together a string of National Old Trails highways, Indian paths, and
railroad spurs. The westering instinct evoked by Irving, Grey, and others
is found here, too, with a dash of futurism. The poem suggests how automobile travel would transform the Midwest, bringing new workers for its
farms and sending its young people out to the plains and the West.*

*Vachel Lindsay was born in Springfield, Illinois, not far from the later
path of Route 66. He was known for his declamatory style in performance
and for titles such as* The Congo and Other Poems *(1914), which includes "The Santa Fe Trail."*

THE SANTA FE TRAIL

I. IN WHICH A RACING AUTO COMES FROM THE EAST

This is the order of the music of the morning:—
First, from the far East comes but a crooning.
The crooning turns to a sunrise singing.
Hark to the calm-horn, balm-horn, psalm-horn.
Hark to the faint-horn, quaint-horn, saint-horn . . .

Its eyes are lamps like the eyes of dragons.
It drinks gasoline from big red flagons.
Butting through the delicate mists of the morning,
It comes like lightning, goes past roaring.
It will hail all the wind-mills, taunting, ringing,
Dodge the cyclones,
Count the milestones,
On through the ranges the prairie-dog tills—
Scooting past the cattle on the thousand hills . . .

II. IN WHICH MANY AUTOS PASS WESTWARD

I want live things in their pride to remain.
I will not kill one grasshopper vain
Though he eats a hole in my shirt like a door.

I let him out, give him one chance more.
Perhaps, while he gnaws my hat in his whim,
Grasshopper lyrics occur to him.

I am a tramp by the long trail's border,
Given to squalor, rags and disorder.
I nap and amble and yawn and look,
Write fool-thoughts in my grubby book,
Recite to the children, explore at my ease,
Work when I work, beg when I please,
Give crank-drawings, that make folks stare
To the half-grown boys in the sunset glare,

And get me a place to sleep in the hay
At the end of a live-and-let-live day.

I find in the stubble of the new-cut weeds
A whisper and a feasting, all one needs:
The whisper of the strawberries, white and red
Here where the new-cut weeds lie dead.

But I would not walk all alone till I die
Without some life-drunk horns going by.

Up round this apple-earth they come
Blasting the whispers of the morning dumb:—
Cars in a plain realistic row.
And fair dreams fade
When the raw horns blow . . .

When houses choke us, and great books bore us!
While I watch the highroad
And look at the sky,
While I watch the clouds in amazing grandeur
Roll their legions without rain
Over the blistering Kansas plain—
While I sit by the milestone
And watch the sky,
The United States
Goes by.

Listen to the iron-horns, ripping, racking.
Listen to the quack-horns, slack and clacking.
Way down the road, trilling like a toad,
Here comes the dice-horn, here comes the vice-horn,
Here comes the snarl-horn, brawl-horn, lewd-horn,
Followed by the prude-horn, bleak and squeaking:—
(Some of them from Kansas, some of them from Kansas) . . .

And all of the tunes, till the night comes down
On hay-stack, and ant-hill, and wind-bitten town.
Then far in the west, as in the beginning,
Dim in the distance, sweet in retreating,

Hark to the faint-horn, quaint-horn, saint-horn,
Hark to the calm-horn, balm-horn, psalm-horn . . .

TOO MANY MIDNIGHTS

CAROLYN WHEAT

– 1928 –

Vachel Lindsey was right: the future belonged to the tooting horn. The excerpt here, from a series of fictional vignettes of Route 66, is a tale of life along Route 66 in the 1920s, the days of Prohibition and the flapper, one of the few such tales told from a female vantage.

In 1926, Route 66 opened to traffic. The Old Trails were not yet Good Roads, but no matter. On the all-weather road, as U.S. 66 was known, one could travel from the great city of Chicago to a distant town where the desert met the Ocean—Los Angeles. The journey might take a month in a fast Packard, or three in a broken-down jalopy.

Formerly a defense attorney, Carolyn Wheat has turned to short fiction. In addition to her own collection of short stories, Tales Out of School *(2000),* Carolyn Wheat *is the editor of* Women Before the Bench *(2001) and the influential compilation of contemporary fiction about Route 66,* Murder on Route 66 *(1998).*

Chicago, Illinois, 1928

"It's the most beautiful dress I've ever seen." Belinda Carlisle couldn't help crushing the crepe to her breast and burying her face in its sheer, bead-bedezened loveliness. "And you're a perfect darling for buying it."

It was her first grown-up dress. The first dress in her life that would allow her legs, freshly shaved and encased in sheer silk stockings, to be the focus of male attention. The days of middy blouses and black lisle hose under demure long skirts were over.

"Oh, Daddy, thank you. Thank you so much." She gave the dress one more loving squeeze and turned toward her bedroom.

"Now, Belinda," her father said, raising his voice, "I want you to promise you won't do anything foolish tonight."

"Oh, no, Papa, I won't." The lie tripped lightly off her tongue, but the dress itself knew she was fibbing. How could anyone not act foolish wearing a cloud of crepe with beads that would gleam in the soft amber light and fringe that would tickle her rouged knees?

Oh, yes. The knees were rouged and so were her cheeks, and she pasted her hair into spit curls on either side of her face and one in the center of her forehead just like Clara Bow. She made a Clara Bow rosebud mouth at herself in the mirror, then broke into a wide innocent smile that showed the gap between her front teeth.

She clamped her lips shut; It Girls didn't have gaps in their teeth like farmer's daughters. They were cool and aloof and mysterious. And tonight she wasn't going to be Belinda Carlisle of the banking Carlisles. She was going to be a flapper, smoking a cigarette in an ivory holder, sipping gin from a silver flask, swearing and smelling of orchids and staying out all night with a college man.

Talking of Paris and F. Scott Fitzgerald and riding in an open roadster with the wind in her hair. She was going to be the kind of woman Daddy wouldn't want her to know.

She loved her father very much, but she wasn't a child anymore, and tonight she was going to prove it.

As she rubbed the rabbit's foot over her face one more time, adding a smidge more rouge, she hummed the new song that was all the rage:

> *You can bring Pearl,*
> *She's a darned nice girl.*
> *But don't bring LuLu.*

> *LuLu always wants to do*
> *What the boys all want her to.*
> *You can bring Sal,*
> *Or Dottie or Al,*
> *But don't bring LuLu.*

When Price introduced her to his friends from college, she said, with a toss of her newly bobbed head, "Oh, don't bother with that old Belinda. Just call me LuLu."

And they did. As the night wore on, as they drove in Price's shiny new car with its leather seats from speakeasy to speakeasy, she gradually became LuLu, shedding bits and pieces of her old Belinda self along the way. The gin helped, of course, but it was the dress that transformed her, somehow permeating her very skin with its forbidden desires.

Finally Price's friend Mack said he knew a place that stayed open all night. A roadhouse. A real and true roadhouse, just like she'd heard about from the fast crowd at school. It was called Wicked Wanda's and it was out on the highway they'd just made a national road. Route 66 it was called, and the sound of it thrilled her because it was so strange and so filled with adventure. It went, or so they said, all the way to Los Angeles, California, and she wondered as they made their way to Joliet how it would feel to keep on going and going and wake up with orange trees all around you.

THE LOST BOY

THOMAS WOLFE

– 1937 –

----

*And now Route 66 moves into the '30s, when Thomas Wolfe was begin-
ning his first novel. The novella excerpted here anticipates the epigraph
to* Look Homeward, Angel, *"a stone, a leaf, an unfound door . . . Which
of us has known his brother? . . . O lost, and by the wind-grieved, ghost,
come back again."*

Wolfe's style here is telegraphic, with multiple narrators. This, like
You Can't Go Home Again, *is a story of a man who tries to return to his
childhood home. In this case, home is St. Louis, which has the trickiest
stretch of Route 66 to navigate because, so the rumor goes, every time the
American Automobile Association moved its headquarters, they rerouted
66 to pass their front door. Today the streetcars are gone from St. Louis,
but traces of them remain among the six alignments of Route 66 there.*

*Thomas Wolfe was one of the stylists of twentieth-century American
literature, known for his trilogy* Look Homeward, Angel; Of Time and
the River; *and* You Can't Go Home Again. *"The Lost Boy" was originally
published in* Redbook *magazine in 1937, in an issue that also featured
original fiction by Sherwood Anderson. (It would be hard to find such
noteworthy literature on a supermarket checkout stand today!)*

Wolfe returned to Route 66 briefly in a trip recorded in his A Western
Journal *in 1938.*

It's all so long ago, as if it happened in another world. And then it all comes back—the boarding-house, St. Louis and the Fair—as if it happened yesterday . . .

I got to thinking of the afternoon we sneaked away from home. . . . Mamma had gone out somewhere. And Robert and I got on the street-car and came downtown. . . . And my Lord, in those days, that was what we called a trip. A ride on the street-car was something to write home about in those days. . . .

So we got on the car and rode the whole way down into the business section of St. Louis. . . . And both of us half scared to death at what we'd done and wondering what Mamma would say if she found out . . .

"This is King's Highway," a man said.

I looked and saw that it was just a street. There were some big new buildings, and a big hotel; some restaurants, "bar-grill" places of the modern kind, the livid monotone of Neon lights, the ceaseless traffic of the motorcars—all this was new, but it was just a street. And I knew that it had always been a street and nothing more. But somehow—I stood there looking at it, wondering what else I had expected to find.

"What line was this?" the man said, and stared at me.

"The interurban line," I said.

Then the man stared at me again and finally, "I don't know no inter-urban line," he said.

I said it was a line that ran behind some houses, and that there were board fences there and grass beside the tracks. But somehow I could not say that it was summer in those days and that you could smell the ties, a wooden, tarry smell, and feel a kind of absence in the afternoon, after the car had gone. I could not say King's Highway had not been a street in those days but a kind of road that wound from magic out of some dim land, and that along the way it had got mixed with Tom the Piper's son, with hot cross buns, with all the light that came and went, and with cloud shadows passing on the mountains, with coming down through Indiana in the morning, and the smell of engine smoke, the Union Station, and most of all with voices lost and far and long ago that said "King's Highway" . . .

It was all so strong, so solid and so ugly—and so enduring and so good, the way I had remembered it, except I did not smell the tar, the hot and caulky dryness of the old cracked ties, the boards of the back-yard fences and the coarse and sultry grass, and absence in the afternoon when the street-car had gone, and the feel of the hot afternoon, and the sense that everyone was absent at the Fair.

It was a hot day. Darkness had come; the heat hung and sweltered like a sodden blanket in St. Louis. The heat soaked down, and people sweltered in it; the faces of the people were pale and greasy with the heat. And in their faces was a kind of patient wretchedness, and one felt the kind of desolation that one feels at the end of a hot day in a great city in America—when one's home is far away across the continent, and he thinks of all that distance, all that heat, and feels: "Oh, God, but it's a big country! . . ."

He feels the way one feels when one comes back, and knows that he should not have come, and when he sees that, after all, King's Highway is—a street; and St. Louis—the enchanted name—a big hot common town upon the river, sweltering in wet dreary heat, and not quite South, and nothing else enough to make it better . . .

And again, again, I turned into the street, finding the place where corners met, turning to look again to see where Time had gone. And all of it was just the same, it seemed that it had never changed since then, except all had been found and caught and captured forever. And so, finding all, I knew all had been lost.

I knew that I would never come again and that lost magic would not come again, and that the light that came, that passed and went and that returned again the memory of lost voices in the hill, cloud shadows passing in the mountains, the voices of our kinsman long ago, the street, the heat, King's Highway, and the piper's son, the vast and drowsy murmur of the distant Fair—oh, strange and bitter miracle of Time—come back again.

THE BOY: OKIE PASSAGE ON ROUTE 66

JAY SMITH

− 1941 −

When a family packed up roots and headed west in the '40s, the wishes of their children rarely figured prominently in their decision. In this next piece, leaving home on Route 66 is told from a boy's point of view, beginning with the great sense of comfort that comes from curling up in the backseat while parents drive through the darkness to a new world. If the boy is unable to run away and return home to Missouri from this 66 voyage, his feelings are nonetheless understandable: the pain of leaving home and friends, the uncertainty at what lies ahead. For many of its younger travelers, Route 66 was not a Mother Road so much as a parents' road, where they were displaced and went along in their family's ambitions. Jay Smith published his account of Okies, Oklahoma migrants, in 1992.

It was chilly in the backseat of the car. I squirmed deeper in my quilt. They got in. The car doors thunked shut. The starter whined and the Pontiac started.

"You got the map?"

"Yes."

"Coffee?"

"Right here."

"Flashlight?"

"Here."

"Cigarettes?"

"Two cartons."

"What time is it?"

The inside of the car lit up when Mother turned on the flashlight. "Three-thirty."

"We're getting an early start."

"I'd say."

The car moved, backed out of the driveway across the short, wooden bridge that creaked and onto the gravel road that crunched. Then we moved forward. Without looking I could see the big house and the little house moving away on the left, dark and ghosty with no lights, trees thick on both sides of the road and around the houses. Past the Elmores' house, down the hill. Up the hill. Around the curve through Roby, past McElroy's Store, past Largent's Store, past Daniel's Store and the Post Office . . .

Dad was a black bulk on the left side of the car, the lights from the dashboard making him a silhouette. He had on a new hat. A fedora, Mother called it. Mother was slumped against the window on the left side. Three people could have fitted in the space between them. She was crying.

I felt like crying but I wasn't going to. I was going to run away. I would wait my chance. They would have to stop sometime. I would slip into the woods and come back. Lassie went home, 900 miles. Twice. And she was a dog. I could do it.

We turned left off Highway 17 onto Highway 32. Dad hit the steering wheel and laughed. "Forty-two miles of rough, rocky road to Lebanon, and then it's concrete all the way to California."

Lebanon was where we hit the slab.

Route 66.

I would slip away and come back. Lebanon wasn't far. Thirty-nine miles. When they stopped at Lebanon, I would slip into the woods. Right now, I would go to sleep. I would sleep all the way to Lebanon.

"Wake up. Wake up and see Kansas."

Mother was reaching over the back of the front seat, pulling at my arm. She was laughing, excited. "The sign said '1 Mile to Kansas State Line.'"

Kansas? I scrambled up and stared out the window. I had slept through Lebanon. If we were to Kansas, we must have gone through Springfield, and Carthage and Joplin. I looked out the back window toward Missouri. White lines in the middle of Route 66 spooled away behind us.

A white sign flashed by. "That's the State Line. We're in Kansas," she announced. I didn't see any line. There were still woods though. I could still slip away. Kansas looked just like Missouri. Hills, trees crowding together in the dark. Good. There were still woods. When I got to the woods, I would be hard to catch.

We were going fast. We had a 1941 Pontiac, dark green. A business coupe, Dad called it. It had an Indian chief on the hood. Chief Pontiac. His face was orange plastic, and when the car's lights were on, Chief Pontiac's face lit. The feathers in his headdress streamed back, a shiny plastic tapering into the middle of the hood, as if he were flying a hundred miles an hour. It felt like we were going a hundred miles an hour. The road wasn't gravel, it was a long white slap of concrete with black tar strips across it. We were flying and the tar strips went "whump" when we hit them. I looked over my father's shoulder at the round speedometer. The red needle was pointing at 60. We were flying.

It was still dark. The orange Indian head pulled us down Route 66. The "whump," "whump," "whump" made me drowsy.

I was almost asleep when Mother pulled my arm again.

"Wake up. Wake up and see Oklahoma." My Mother, excited again. Kansas must be tiny. Another State Line without a line. A white sign flashed by.

"How far are we from Missouri?"

"Not far from the state line."

"How far from Lebanon?"

Mother handed me a small orange book.

"Here. Look it up."

It was A *Guidebook to Highway 66* by Jack D. Rittenhouse. On the front was a drawing of a stagecoach going past a big cactus. Lebanon to Springfield was 51 miles. Springfield to Carthage, 61 miles, 17 more miles to Joplin and 20 more miles to the Oklahoma State Line. 149 miles. My heart sank.

We were in Oklahoma. There were fewer trees, and no hills. It was light, but light without sun. OK, I had missed Lebanon; I had missed Springfield. I could still slip away. It would just take longer, that's all. I would be patient and wait my chance.

BLIND CORNER

DAVID AUGUST

— 1950s —

Travelers tend to focus on the extremities of Route 66, the edge of the continent near the Pacific or the tall buildings of downtown Chicago. Yet a third of the way across its length, in the Ozark Mountains, they encounter some of its most remote and twisty sections. This is "Dangerous 66," as Skip Curtis of Missouri called it.

The Ozarks have always been a region rent by turmoil. After the Civil War, this was where Quantrill's Raiders stormed as renegades, as neither Southern nor Northern troops, owing allegiance only to themselves. Then the first decades of the twentieth century exploded with racial tension. Despite the out-migration of African Americans, such tensions have hung over from the nineteenth into the twenty-first.

This is another story told from a boy's point of view, set in the 1950s in the dark, heavily wooded stretch of Route 66, near the twist they call "Dead Man's Curve." There are legends of Ozarkers who made their living picking up the pieces from accidents in this most-sinuous stretch of the Old Road. (Sometimes, it's whispered, they weren't above leaving a log on the road to help business along.) There is a gothic flavor to the story that follows, reflecting the tension between those who lived in these hills and hollers, and those for whom it was only a throughway.

David August was raised in St. Louis, not far from the Mother Road itself. He is the coauthor of the thriller Final Seconds *(1998). Writing without his pseudonym, David Linzee is the author of such novels as*

Death in Connecticut *(1978)*, Discretion *(1979)*, Belgravia *(1979)*, *and* Housebreaker *(1987)*.

J ust outside the town of Palenville, where Route 66 shed the name of Main Street and became itself again, it ran into Blake's Hill. This was southern Missouri, the foothills of the Ozarks, and the country was rugged. Blake's Hill was too steep to go over and too big to blast through, so they'd bent 66 around it. The road took a sharp left followed by a fish-hook right.

The way the men at the volunteer fire department told it, the curve began to get its bad reputation when Dr. Stiller had his accident there. The Doc spun out and bounced back and forth from hillside to guardrail, wrecking his brand-new 1946 Buick Roadmaster and putting himself in a bed in his own hospital for a month.

But it wasn't till the Drew Blackmer crash that people started calling the turn Dead Man's Curve. Drew went off the road and rolled his '52 Chevy pickup four times. They had to cut his body out of the cab with an acetylene torch.

The volunteer firemen would tell such stories for hours to the boys who liked to hang around the station after school. There were plenty of accidents to talk about. Dwayne Becker, who drove the hook-and-ladder truck, even said that the song "Crash and Burn" by Todd and the Styletones was based on an accident that had taken place on Dead Man's Curve. A teenager came around the blind corner too fast, in the wrong lane, and ran head-on into another car, and she'd been killed. In the chorus he begged the Lord to let him change places with her. Some of the firemen scoffed and said no such accident had ever happened around here, but Dwayne listened to the song on his transistor all the time, and he could quote the lyrics. The description of the blind corner matched the curve around Blake's Hill to a T.

The boys wanted to believe Dwayne, especially Zachary Woodrell. Zack was a bright and talkative twelve-year-old, and he'd remind the doubters of what it was like during the summer vacation months. Every time you came to the Curve, you'd find yourself at the back of a long line of cars with out-of-state plates, inching along with their brake lights flashing. It had to be the worst turn the tourists met up with on the whole length of 66, Zack said. Even in Los Angeles, where the people who made up the songs lived, they must know about Dead Man's Curve in Palenville, Missouri.

Zack's mom didn't want to listen to that kind of talk. She thought that there were a lot of other things in Palenville a boy should feel proud of, instead of a bad turn in the road. Maybe Zack shouldn't hang around the firehouse so much, she said, hearing stories about injury and death and getting a kick out of them. He wouldn't think Dead Man's Curve accidents were so much fun, if he ever saw one.

One day in March of '58, Zack's mom got her wish.

It had snowed so heavily the night before that school was closed that day. Zack and his friends spent the afternoon fighting a fierce snowball battle, Yankees versus Rebels, and Zack had fun even though they made him be on the Yankee side. At four o'clock, feeling weary and chilled, he was trudging along the flank of Blake's Hill toward home. He wasn't thinking about anything except dinner . . .

The screech of tires made him stop in his tracks. He shivered as if somebody'd slipped an iceball down his back. It sounded like the scream of an animal in pain, even though he knew it was really a car skidding. It went on and on.

It was coming from the other side of the hill. From Dead Man's Curve.

The car was still sliding when it came around the turn. It was one that would have caught Zack's eye even if it had been standing still—a Thunderbird, silver with a black convertible top. The hood airscoop and basketwork grille told him that it was the new '58 model, the one Richard Diamond, private eye, drove on TV. It didn't belong to anybody from around here. There weren't many convertibles in Palenville. Zack had never even ridden in one, never felt the wind in his hair.

It looked as if the car was going to skid off the road but at the last moment the driver straightened it out. The screeching of its tires ceased. It accelerated as it came toward Zack. The front end was dented and one of the headlights was smashed.

The car shot past him. He swiveled to look after it. The license plate was black with orange lettering. Out-of-state. Squinting, he was able to read the numbers in the moment before the T-bird roared away: 713-WXM.

He shut his eyes. There were too many letters and numbers for him to remember. He felt as if he were carrying something that was too heavy for him. He was staggering and his grip was slipping.

Opening his eyes Zack looked down at the snow. He bent and wrote the license number in it with his gloved fingers.

He straightened up, relieved. Now there was time to think. The guy in the T-bird must have hit another car. Instead of stopping, he'd stepped on the gas. But he wasn't going to get away. Zack had him.

WEST ON 66

JAMES H. COBB

— 1950s —

Route 66 does a dogleg through the very southeast corner of Kansas between Joplin, Missouri, and Vinita, Oklahoma. The stretch, though only
13.2 miles, is packed with legends and history, from mysterious "Spook
Lights," floating globes of heat lightning over the swamps, to ghostly
memories of Civil War battles and cattle drives. This small section of
Kansas combines two different traditions: Kansas as a land of cowboys
and cattle, and Kansas as a zinc and lead mining center, which continued until the bypassing of Route 66 in the 1980s.

This next selection runs past the tri-state area's artificial mountains
of chat, detritus from the mines that leaches into the ground. Here, 66
passes over the Neosho River, which has been known to run orange from
the chemical debris that washes up from abandoned mines. Today it's not
a happy country. The nearby town of Picher, Oklahoma, is under evacua-
tion in its entirety for contamination.

In this contemporary novel, the reader finds film noir's cousin, roman
noir: another story of a hard-boiled cop and a long chase—across Route
66 in this case—searching for clues to a missing mob fortune.

James H. Cobb has always been fascinated by the U.S. Navy; he's a
member of the U.S. Naval Institute and author of a series of thrillers at
sea, Sea Strike (1998), Sea Fighter (2000), and Target Lock (2002). His
thriller, West on 66 (1999), features an east–west journey of discovery.

We knocked off the last hundred miles to the Kansas-Missouri line before eleven the next morning. There's not much of 66 in Kansas, just a short hook through the very southeastern corner of the state. You could drive it in a quarter of an hour if it weren't for the two towns, Galena and Baxter Springs, that you have to pass through.

This little patch of land was soaked in a lot of history though, history and blood, the two being frequently synonymous. The Jayhawkers had ridden here before the Civil War, Quantrill's Raiders during, and the James gang after. And there had been later incarnations as well.

Galena was the mining town, and at the peak of the lead and zinc boom its main drag had been called the Red Hot Street. It had burned bright on Saturday nights as the miners came roaring in to dump their pay into the pockets of the pimps, tinhorns, and barkeeps.

Later had come the depression and the strikes. I could remember Dad talking about the bad times in Galena. In a struggle between rival miners' groups, nine CIO organizers had been gunned down in the streets, and the National Guard had been brought in to declare things a draw.

As for Baxter Springs, it had been the destination of the first herds of Texas longhorns to flow up the Chisholm Trail after the Civil War. Dodge City, Abilene, and all the other hell-raising Kansas cow towns that came later just followed the example that had been set here.

Now the cattle drives were gone, replaced by the big mid-western truck fleets that used Baxter as a home terminal. And the mines were playing out, leaving nothing behind in Galena except for grim stories and gritty gray mounds of ore tailing. Chat heaps, the locals called them. Both communities were sinking into a peaceful Middle America sleepiness.

Barring the odd corpse that still turned up now and again.

"I tried calling ahead from the motel this morning," Lisette said over the road wind fluttering through the '57's windows. Route 66 had just crossed a one-lane rainbow arc bridge and now almost tunneled through a thick and humid grove of blackjack and ground cherry. "That number in the guidebook isn't good anymore. They've changed over to a whole new directory system. And directory assistance doesn't list a Claster anywhere in either Baxter Springs or Galena."

"That doesn't mean all that much, Princess," I replied. ". . . Claster might not have a phone, or he might be living in a rooming house or an apartment. Even if this Jubal guy's moved on, there's got to be somebody around here who'll know something."

Lisette peered at me over the top of my commandeered sunglasses. "And how do we go about finding this somebody?"

"We ask. Hell, it's not like this place is Chicago. In a small town, everybody knows everybody. Even in a middlin' big small town like Baxter Springs, enough people are going to know enough people so it shouldn't be that big of a deal. Trust me."

I took a second glance across at her. "Haven't you ever spent any time in a small town?"

"Gary was the smallest. And I didn't know a lot of people."

She went cold, silently warning me off the subject. Just like every other time I'd tried to probe into her past. The hatches would slam shut, and her wariness would return.

I let it ride as we blew past the sign welcoming us to Baxter Springs . . .

The service station was set in a patch of weeds and rusty car hulks. An army surplus Quonset hut with a couple of wood frame add-ons, its white paint losing the fight to a growing collection of rust stains. Turning into the shale rock driveway, I stopped the '57 just short of the bell house. It was getting late in the day, and the sun was edging below a hazy horizon. Back up in the tanglewood, katydids screeched a protest against the heat.

"This is it, Princess; here's where we find the guy we need to talk to."

Galena, Kansas

The Round Barn, Arcadia, Oklahoma

PLAINS 66

OKLAHOMA AND TEXAS

WORKING WITH WILL

GREG MALAK

− 1930s −

In the early days, Route 66 was called the Will Rogers Highway. This was not just because he was born a few miles outside of Claremore, Oklahoma, on Route 66, but also because he spent a good part of his life driving 66 or flying over it in his own plane. Will Rogers was Route 66's most famous traveler.

Northeast Oklahoma is still Rogers Country. The 66 traveler today can drive south toward Oklahoma City either on the Will Rogers Highway or the Will Rogers Turnpike. The road will take him past Rogers State University, the Will Rogers airport, and the Will Rogers Memorial Museum, which Greg Malak has directed. Will Rogers was known for saying, "I never met a man I didn't like."

Greg Malak spent thirty years sharing his ever-growing knowledge with interested museum patrons and researchers as a staffer and associate director of the Will Rogers Memorial Museum. When he retired from the museum, he was awarded the Will Rogers Communicator Award for his dedication (an award first given to Ronald Reagan).

The Will Rogers Memorial Museum artfully displays facets of his career: Will Rogers on radio and on film. Will Rogers the pilot. Will Rogers the columnist. Will Rogers the star of Wild West shows, roping anything within his reach. After decades of working with Will, Greg Malak gives the reader an overview of the dramatic career of Route 66's native son.

W ill Rogers was born about twelve miles north of Claremore. That was Indian Territory, back well over one hundred years ago. Both his mother and father are part Cherokee Indian, and he was raised in that environment. Grew up when it was wilderness, rather rough living out here, but he went from there and reached great heights in everything he did. Route 66 was dirt then, and going from Claremore or Tulsa down to Oklahoma City on Route 66—well, if there was a lot of rain, you were stuck.

Rogers left school, traveled around the world, took up with rodeos, wild west shows, had success there. From there he went into vaudeville, became a headliner. He was a headliner for the Ziegfeld Follies. From there it was just natural to go into movies. He worked for Fox Studios, 1933–1935. He was the number one male box-office star, outdrawing everyone else.

He also had a weekly radio show. Most people remember the one he did for Gulf Radio on Sunday evenings. Originally it conflicted with church. So many pastors got in touch: they said people are staying at home listening to you on the radio instead of coming to church. So he changed the time. Of course, he didn't want to interfere with church. He was published nationally in 650 newspapers, weekly and daily, and his wit and wisdom still pertains.

He traveled this country many, many times—traversed it.

Later, the highway later became known as Route 66 but prior to that it was the Will Rogers Highway, and one that he traveled extensively. He would travel it not only for show business but to do relief tours to help needy folks.

Out in California it is interesting that where Route 66 ends there is a plaque to Will Rogers. What he stood for—the common sense, the hard work, the honesty, all those things—I think still exist today on the highway. It's a reawakening of folks wanting to travel the highway because you want to get back to your roots and find out what really is important here in America. And Route 66 is that road.

Will Rogers Memorial Museum

THE AUTOBIOGRAPHY
OF WILL ROGERS

WILL ROGERS

– 1926 –

Will Rogers's career is bracketed by Route 66, from the road he took to his many elementary schools to the theater in San Bernardino where he gave his last performance. His autobiography was a best seller, for Rogers embodied America during the Great Depression. He was seen on the Saturday matinee and heard on the radio. His writing is folksy with a vengeance, replete with eccentric spellings and hokum. This style spoke to the vast number of people in transit, reminding them of the way things used to be back home, the old days, and the folks left behind. Will Rogers was also one of the first Indians to win national acclaim. In his day, he kept company with presidents. This excerpt gives voice to the man and legend after whom the highway was first named.

William Penn Adair Rogers was born in 1879 in the Indian Territory and died in 1935. In addition to careers as a newspaper columnist, a radio and film star (he made seventy-one films), and a roping champion, he wrote six books in a cracker-barrel vein, including The Illiterate Digest *(1924) and* There's Not a Bathing Suit in Russia *(1927).*

Claremore is the county seat of Rogers County, which was named for my father. My family had lived there for over fifty years. My father was one-eighth Cherokee Indian and my mother was a quarter-blood Cherokee. I never got far enough in arithmetic to figure out just how much "Injun" that makes me, but there's nothing of which I am more proud than my Cherokee blood. My father was a senator in the tribe for years, and was a member of the convention that drafted the constitution of the State of Oklahoma.

My father was pretty well fixed, and I being the only male son he tried terribly hard to make something out of me. He sent me to about every school in that part of the country. In some of them I would last for three or four months. I got just as far as the fourth reader when the teachers wouldn't seem to be running the school right, and rather than have the school stop I would generally leave.

"Drumgoul" was a little one-room log cabin four miles east of Chelsea, Indian Territory (where I am right now writing). It was all Indian kids went there and I being part Cherokee had enough white in me to make my honesty questionable.

There must have been about thirty of us in that room that had rode horseback and walked miles to get there, and by the way it was a Co-Ed Institution. About half of 'em was Coo-Coo Eds. We graduated when we could print our full names and enumerate to the teacher, or Principal or Faculty (well, whenever we could name to her), the nationality of the last Democratic President . . .

The lariat-slinging business drifted into my system when I was pretty young. My father would send me out on the ranch, but instead of riding the range I'd go off into a shady place and there spend the time practicing with the rope-cutting curliques and things in the prairie breeze or lassoing prairie dogs and things not made to be lassoed.

Then he hired me out to other ranch-men, but I was so fond of using the lariat when there was no call for it that I couldn't hold a job. In a fit of bad temper the old gent decided to make a preacher of me, and sent me to a school up in Missouri. When I lassoed the stone gal— goddess of something—off the top of the water fountain and broke all her limbs, the old gent paid the bill rather than have me sent back to the nation, because he didn't need me on the ranch, but when I got the string around the Professor's neck—by accident—my career on the road to the ministry ended . . .

Well, my old dad called me off a few weeks later and told me, "If you're bound to punch cows, there's no need for you to leave home. You're the only child I have at home now, as your sisters are married and have homes of their own. I'm going to give you this Dog Iron Ranch, lock, stock, and barrel. It's yours and you can run it the way you want to, for I'm going to move to Claremore."

Well, I didn't run it to suit him. I danced all my young life to the music of old country fiddlers and I didn't drag a bad bow myself. Between dances and roping contests, I didn't have time for much serious ranching business.

My real show career kinder dates from the time I first run into the Col. Zack Mulhall. It was in 1899 at the St. Louis fair (not the World's fair, just the big St. Louis fair they held every year). They had decided as an attraction that they would put on a Roping and Riding Contest. They were not called Rodeos or Stampedes, in those days they were just what they are, a "Roping and Riding Contest." Well I was pretty much of a Kid, but had just happened to have won the first and about my only Contest at home in Claremore, Okla., and then we read about them wanting entries for this big contest at St. Louis.

Well some one sent in my name, and the first thing I knew I was getting transportation for myself and pony to the affair. Well I went, and Col. Zack Mulhall had charge of it. I didn't get very far in this St. Louis Contest. I made the serious mistake of catching my steer and he immediately jerked me and my Pony down for our trouble.

But that gave me a touch of "Show business" in a way, so that meant I was ruined for life as far as actual employment was concerned.

BACK ROAD 66

LANCE HENSON

– 1960s –

As it crosses the dusty plains of Oklahoma, Route 66 passes through the unified lands of the Cheyenne and Arapaho tribes. The Cheyenne, agrarians from the upper Midwest, and the Arapaho, nomads from Montana, Wyoming, and Colorado, came to present-day Oklahoma long before Route 66 was even dreamed of. Today, the Old Road runs through El Reno, Oklahoma, one of the population centers for the state's Cheyenne. Drive a few miles west on 66 from El Reno and then a few more north on a country road and you'll reach Calumet, where poet Lance Henson spent his childhood and adolescence.

Henson's vision of 66 is far removed from that of tourists and nostalgics. Growing up on the back roads of 66, Henson experienced the thrill of the open road and the romance of the American West, but also the aftermath of nineteenth-century religious persecution of his people, and the irony of seeing ancestral corridors transformed into asphalt roadways. Henson's story illustrates the complex relationship between American Indians and Route 66: the road brought greater mobility and new economic opportunities, but also further compromised the territorial sovereignty of ancestral lands and at times rendered the Indian a spectacle for gawking tourists.

Henson's twenty-eight books of poetry have been translated into at least twenty-five languages. In 2000 and 2006 he initiated a tour of native poets in Europe, bringing together indigenous poets from India, New Zealand, and the United States. He has been a poet-in-residence at the

Millay Colony for the Arts as well as the University of New Mexico, and was named to the Alumni Hall of Fame at his alma mater, the University of Science and Arts of Oklahoma.

I was raised in the Calumet, Oklahoma, community (nineteen miles northwest of El Reno). The highway that branches off old Route 66 branches into Calumet. It was almost a daily-traveled road for me as a child and as a teenager driving on Route 66.

Then the TV series—my family was one of the first families in the Cheyenne region to have a television, and the Route 66 TV series was one of the programs that we would literally flock around to see—here are these cool guys in adventures in a Corvette down Route 66.

If you travel from El Reno to Clinton, Oklahoma, on Route 66, you will cross the South Canadian River. Right where the bridge is, where the old road crosses the river, is a wide expanse of a river (though it's nearly a stream now). There is a little valley that comes out of Geary, Oklahoma, and it was a travel route of my people when they would go to visit other tribes. They would literally cross the river there, where the old bridge is. If you look at the landscape you can see that it was a place for a river crossing, right where the bridge of Route 66 is.

If you follow that route, it goes up into an area called Twelve-Mile Point, where the creek tributary goes into the North Canadian River. There our people camped and crossed over. When the medicine people came with our medicine, and we were placed in the Indian Territory, that's where our medicine was placed. It's where in 1901 the first hidden Sundance of my people took place. (The Sundance was outlawed from 1901–1903.) This river valley is where the Sundance was hidden from the soldiers, just a few miles from the old highway that would be 66.

That road became, in my older high school days, a road where a lot of my friends lived. We would drive up and down that highway.

In the 1960s, it became a safe road for Indians without drivers' licenses. There was the interstate, and there was this road. Highway Patrol would rarely patrol it so it was one of the Indian roads that people would use to get to Clinton and to other areas where you would rarely be stopped. There are a lot of Cheyenne who even today don't have drivers' licenses—it's sort of a way we rebel against the system. That was the thrill of it.

WILD BOY OF THE ROAD

KAREN HESSE

– 1934 and 1935 –

Route 66 was a road of flight but it was also a road of family, which makes the next excerpt all the more poignant. This poem is the story of a boy, thin as a pole and forced to set out on his own, without his family, traveling west to God knows where.

Much has been written of the ancient vehicles that carried migrants from Oklahoma. It's instructive to remember that those who couldn't afford a jalopy still managed to find their way out of the Dust Bowl—by walking Route 66. In this and other accounts of the Okies' transit, California shimmers like Eden, a lush, green place where work was to be had, where the sun shone, and, as Jimmie Rodgers sang in his "California Blues," "where they sleep out every night." But getting there could be tough on your shoes.

Karen Hesse is the author of ten books for children, including the award-winning The Music of Dolphins *(1996). Her poetry collection* Out of the Dust *(1997), which includes "Wild Boy of the Road," won a Newberry Award. Although her books and poems are addressed to children, their gravity often asks for adult understanding and contemplation.*

A boy came by the house today,
he asked for food.
He couldn't pay anything, but Ma set him down
and gave him biscuits
and milk.
He offered to work for his meal,
Ma sent him out to see Daddy.
The boy and Daddy came back late in the afternoon.
The boy walked two steps behind,
in Daddy's dust.
He wasn't more than sixteen.
Thin as a fence rail.
I wondered what
Livie Killian's brother looked like now.
I wondered about Livie herself.
Daddy asked if the boy wanted a bath,
a haircut,
a change of clothes before he moved on.
The boy nodded.
I never heard him say more than "Yes, sir" or
"No, sir" or
"Much obliged."

We watched him walk away
down the road,
in a pair of Daddy's mended overalls,
his legs like willow limbs,
his arms like reeds.
Ma rested her hands on her heavy stomach,
Daddy rested his chin on the top of my head.
"His mother is worrying about him," Ma said.
"His mother is wishing her boy would come home."

Lots of mothers wishing that these days,
while their sons walk to California,
where rain comes,
and the color green doesn't seem like such a miracle,
and hope rises daily, like sap in a stem.

And I think, some day I'm going to walk there too,
through New Mexico and Arizona and Nevada.
Some day I'll leave behind the wind, and the dust
and walk my way West
and make myself to home in that distant place
of green vines and promise.

THE NEGRO MOTORIST GREEN BOOK

VICTOR H. GREEN

– 1936 –

Recognizing the need for a travel guide telling where African Americans could eat and stay in segregated America, Green's guide made travel easier and benefited African American businesses. Green's motto was "Carry the Green Book with you . . . you may need it." Following in the footsteps of Jewish guidebooks, he documented establishments that welcomed African American patrons to their business. The success of the guide is evidenced by its humble beginnings as a local guide for New York City and its subsequent expansion to a national and international publication.

The guide itself is essentially a listing, like a telephone book, with very little narrative. The publishers request corrections or comments but state explicitly that they cannot make any recommendations. The underlying rhetoric in this disclaimer as well as the guide's frequent use of terms like "embarrassment" or "inconvenience" highlights the very real discomfort and danger African Americans faced traveling beyond familiar neighborhoods and towns—where their mobility clashed with Jim Crow brutality. A postal carrier and travel agent, Victor H. Green published his guide in 1936 and continued it for at least two decades.

Throughout the ages, men of all races have moved from place to place. Some to seek new lands, others to avoid persecution or intolerance, and still others for the sake of adventure. Today, men of all races continue to move and for much the same reasons, though since the days of the foot-traveler and the ox-cart, they travel with much more convenience and at far greater speed.

For most travelers, whether they travel in modern high-speed motor cars, streamlined Diesel-powered trains, luxurious ocean liners or globe encircling planes, there are hotels of all sizes and classes, waiting and competing for their patronage. Pleasure resorts in the mountains and at the sea shore beckon him. Roadside inns and cabins spot the highways and all are available if he has the price.

For some travelers however, the facilities of many of these places are not available, even though they may have the price, and any traveler to whom they are not available, is thereby faced with many and sometimes difficult problems.

The Negro traveler's inconveniences are many and they are increasing because today so many more are traveling, individually and in groups.

There will be a day sometime in the near future when this guide will not have to be published. That is when we as a race will have equal opportunities and privileges in the United States. It will be a great day for us to suspend this publication for then we can go wherever we please, and without embarrassment. But until that time comes we shall continue to publish this information for your convenience each year.

'53 BUICK

GARY PHILLIPS

− 1955 −

This next tale is a story of DWB (Driving While Black) after World War II. Route 66 was not always a pleasant trip for those who traveled it. For much of Route 66's history, the road passed through a segregated landscape, where water coolers and restrooms were marked "Whites Only." Blacks had to carry a list of motels, such as Green's guide, where they could spend the night in a segregated town, or where they could get dinner or a soda pop without having to walk to the back door.

The driver in the next selection comes from one of the small but independent black towns that existed in the American Southwest, such as Boley, Oklahoma. One was actually set up on Route 66: North Amarillo Heights—where a black cowboy decided his people needed a place of their own—was on Route 66 in Texas. Toni Morrison has written about these communities in her novel Paradise: the fear and isolation African Americans had, and the danger of traveling along isolated roads. This story reminds us that such fears were not just fiction, and the magic of Route 66 was no protection against racism.

Gary Phillips is the author of nine volumes, many of them mysteries set in Las Vegas, such as High Hand (2000) and Shooter's Point (2001). He has written about the 1992 Los Angeles race riot and even has two comic book series (Angeltown and Midnight Mover).

Barreling out of Amarillo, the sandstorm swooped in just as Dolphy Ornette steered the black and red 1953 Buick Roadmaster directly into its path. Route 66 lay flat and hard and open before him like a whore he knew back home in Boley, Oklahoma. Some Friday nights men would be stepping all over each other in the service porch off her rear bedroom, waiting their turn.

He'd bought the car two years ago when he'd cashiered out of Korea with his corporal's wages. He'd fought a war just like his older brother had not more than a decade before. Of course, just as with that war, the downtown white men suddenly got a lot of "we" and "us" in their speeches, and told the colored boys it was their duty to go protect freedom. His brother didn't make it back from the war.

Back in '42 the enemy were krauts and nips. In '51 they were the goddamn gooks. White man always could come up with colorful names for everybody else except himself. Dinge, shine, jig, smoke, coon, even had dago, wop, mick, kike for those whites who talked their English with an accent or ate food that they definitely didn't serve down at the corner diner.

The NAACP also said negroes should fight, prove they were loyal Americans and that they could face 'em down with the best of them. So they soldiered up. Surely that would show the ofays back home, things would have to improve in housing and jobs once our boys got back. The black soldiers who returned with the memories of lost lives and innocence and blood had the nerve to demand what was theirs from the big boss man. Now boy, things is going back the ways they always was. Sure Truman integrated the troops in Korea, but that was war time. This was peace.

A steady hammering of sand rapped against his windshield. Earlier, before the break of dawn, he could tell what was coming as he stood gassing the Buick at the dilapidated station in McLean. The old Confederate who ran the place wasn't inclined to sell him gas, but business wasn't exactly knocking down his weather-beaten door, so a few colored dollars would do him.

The wind off the Panhandle drove the sand at the glass with the fine consistency that reminded him of the sound when his mama fried up cornmeal in a pan. But the car's road-devouring V-8 and the Twin-Turbine Dynaflow torque converter kept the machine steady and on course across the blacktop. He was glad he'd paid extra for the power steering, even though at the time he did think it was a mite sissified. The twelve-volt charging unit was doing its job. The dash lights didn't dim like his DeSoto's used to do.

He drove on and on with the sandstorm ranging around his car like the song of one of those sea mermaids luring you. Like you'd get so hot to be with her you wouldn't notice until it was too late as a giant squid popped the eyes out of your head as it squeezed your ribcage together.

Dolphy Ornette kept driving, periodically glancing at the broken yellow line dotting the center of the two-lane highway. The pelting sand sounded a lullaby of nature's indifference to humanity. He drove on because he needed to put distance between himself and where he'd left, and because he needed to get where he was going. Not that he thought they'd suspect him. No, the big boss man couldn't conceive of a black man being that clever. A couple of them might wonder what had put it in his head to quit. But he'd waited weeks after filching the doohickey to announce he was going back to Boley.

Anyway the generals and the chrome dome boys would be too busy trying to figure out how the dirty reds had stolen the gizmo. A blast of wind, like the swipe of a giant's backhand, caused the front end of his car to swerve viciously to the right. His hands tightened on the wheel, and he managed to keep the Roadmaster under control. Ornette slowed his speed to compensate for the turbulence. It wouldn't do to flip over now.

He should'a rotated the tires before he left, but he had other matters to deal with. Up ahead, an old Ford F-1 truck with rusted fenders weaved to and fro. The trailer attached to it shimmied like one of those plastic hula girls he'd seen in the rear window of hot rods.

Ornette slowed down, watching the taillights of the trailer blink through the sheet of brown blur swirling before him. It sounded as if a thousand snares in a room full of drums were being beat. The red lights before him swayed and jerked. On he drove through the gale until it was no more, and all that remained was a night with pinholes for stars, and a silver crescent of a moon hanging like it was on a string. He pulled over somewhere the hell in New Mexico. Using the flashlight, he checked the windshield. The glass was pitted and several spiderweb cracks like children's pencil marks worked at the edges. But the metal molding seemed intact. He tapped the butt of the flashlight against the windshield in several places and it held. He popped the hood to check the hoses and then cleaned away the grit on the radiator with a whisk broom he took from the glove compartment. Looking toward a series of lights, Ornette figured he'd take a chance and see if he could get accommodations. He had a copy of *The Negro Motorist Green Book* in the glove box. It was the black traveler's guide to hospitable lodging, and to which lodging was to be avoided.

At the moment, Dolphy Ornette was too tired and too ornery to give a damn. As he drove closer he could see a neon sign of a cowgirl straddling a rocket with a saddle around its midsection. Blinking yellow lightning bolts zig-zagged out like a series of movie rockets had landed tail first in the dirt. The place was called the Blast-Off Motor Lodge. Beneath the girl on the sign was a smaller sign announcing cocktails. If they rented him a room, they'd probably take his money for scotch, he wistfully concluded. He patted the trunk and walked inside.

BLACK ON 66

EDMOND THREATT

– 1980s –

This is the account of a hard-working African American veteran trying to find that promise, a piece of the American dream and a way to live decently along Route 66 in white America. For half a century, America has been driving by Edmond Threatt's front door. Many a Route 66 traveler has waved at him as he sat on his riding mower in tiny Luther, Oklahoma. But few have stopped and learned his story—how his family gave the land to build Route 66 through here, from the 160 acres they had homesteaded. How he and his brothers as young children had sat on a hill and watched the trucks plowing and grading a road for the rest of America to drive. And how, despite serving his country in the armed services and working in schools and volunteering his time to civic groups, he has had difficulties in finding a place to be buried, for even in recent times, in central Oklahoma, blacks and whites do not lie together in the cemetery.

Edmond Threatt has not had much formal education, but the man is learned. (His town closed down the black high school after desegregation and barely allowed him into the new one.) Yet Threatt sees hope in the future of race relations along Route 66. In the Navy, and in his local schools, Threatt worked for his country and his community. His life story is dark, but not bleak. Ironically, he was named for a nearby "sundown" town (Edmond, Oklahoma) where blacks could not stop.

I was born about a half mile up here in the woods in a log cabin: July the sixth, 1922. My dad came here from Harpersville, Alabama, and he settled here back in the 1900s, I guess. I don't know when. Him and my momma, they moved here and they got this land right in here. They had 160 acres.

Route 66 wasn't ripped down here but about a half mile or less. It cut through and come on part of our property, and we would run up there and see all the cars and trucks and things. They would let us off down there and we used to run up here on the highway. I was talking to a guy the other day in Luther there, 'bout how we used to run up there on 66 highway and peel that tar off the cracks there and chew it for chewing gum (laughs).

We didn't have nothing but wagons or nothing. Horses then. Around here people grew cotton, corn, peanuts, sweet potatoes, peas. My dad—I forgot what year it was—but he told us he was going to buy him a Model T if we made a good cotton crop that year. And we picked cotton and picked cotton and we raised 32 bales of cotton in one year. And the next year he bought a car. A Model T Ford.

There was eleven of us. Some don't believe it. But I remember we used to take crowcakes to school made out of black-eyed peas and put some eggs in it cause we had plenty eggs, plenty chickens. Squeeze all that juice out and put some eggs in there and other ingredients like you do in crowcakes. Good! Because we were poor. Just what on the farm we had. We had to shell corn, grind corn for cornbread. Sometimes we'd take it to the mill in Luther there—there were two mills there in Luther—and then we'd sift it up and make some flour out of it.

I went to Booker T. Washington High School. That's in Luther. They torn the building down now, when they integrated it back in the '50s. Today black people live all around.

White people and black people aren't buried together. Not around here. They got their own cemeteries. Like the Brown funeral home man told me the other day, some uppity people, white people here in Luther, told him that if they'd a-knew that he was going to bury negro peoples, they wouldn't have let him move in Luther. What do you think of that?

Brown, the funeral home guy, said if somebody want to be buried, and they ain't got no place to put 'em, he gonna help 'em get a spot over there at the Luther cemetery. The white cemetery. And it may be buried right side of your momma. He said it'll never happen.

There was a sign before you got to Edmond, "Don't Let the Sun Set on You in This Town," right down the road, about a mile and a half. If blacks had some property in Edmond, they would burn 'em out and wouldn't let them rebuild. They put a sign there and said, "We had the Health Department up to check your house. It's not livable. You can't live there no more." And then, they give him a few dollars for it.

I went up to the train there to pick up my sister. I was waiting. And I went in the café there to get me a sandwich. And they told me to come around the back. I said, "No, forget it." And I went on out the door. And my sister and cousin and more people in the car told me to hurry up and let's get out of there.

I said, "No, I'm not gonna run. I'm gonna just take my time and get to my vehicle."

And then the police stopped me trying to get out of town. He asked me, "What's wrong, boy?"

"Whatcha mean," I said.

"You're stirring up a little peace in this town."

I said, "Well, I wasn't stirring up no peace. I asked for them to go and get me a sandwich, get us something to eat and something to drink for all of us and they wanted me to go around to the back. And I thought this was America and I didn't think it was that Jim Crow and prejudiced at places. You wasn't begging for nothing. You didn't ask nobody to give you nothin' free."

He said, "Well, you better get out of town."

I said, "I'm going. Another thing, how old do peoples get when you stop calling them 'boys'?"

There's hope. Lots of peoples right down this road, married, black and white. And they are nice people and they go to church together. I don't think they go around here.

The next generation is more open. 'Cause they play football together. They're playing football and running and going to school together and riding, laughing, and hugging each other. I was down last week getting food. One of the white girls, some black guy went over there and took a bite off her sandwich. I saw some peoples frowning up at them. I sat there in my car just looking. I said, "Now I hope something isn't going to break out here." The kids laughed and let him.

MR. ROUTE 66

MICHAEL WALLIS

— 2000 —

More than any other contemporary author, Michael Wallis, with his twice-published volume The Mother Road, *returned Route 66 to American attention—after the trough into which it fell following its popularity during the Route 66 television series in the 1960s.*

Wallis is a stem-winding speaker, who may yet run for political office. If he is elected, it will be on a ticket of the kind of economic renovation that Oklahoma has found in publicizing its stretch of the Mother Road, including in its Route 66 museum in Clinton, Oklahoma, and a new center in Tulsa. Few writers on the road are so well known as Wallis, author of fifteen books about the West, including one on Billy the Kid and another on the Lincoln Highway. Wallis has spoken on Route 66 so many times, driven down so many stretches in the company of everyone from ambassadors to Harley-Davidson cyclists, that he sees Route 66 in his mind's eye when he closes his eyes. He grasps it in its entirety, across time, across place. After all these years, he can still find time to talk to a roadie who has discovered his address and presumed to ring him up or push his doorbell. Almost no one goes away from meeting Michael Wallis without sharing in his love of Route 66.

This highway really is like a mirror held up to the nation. And I do think it reflects who we are, where we've been, and in a way where we're going: sometimes the reflection is good, sometimes it's a bit cloudy, sometimes it's ugly. It's a bittersweet journey for some people.

It's not always been a pleasant ride. Thank God this is not Disneyland. This is the real world, on Route 66. Let's face it, not every traveler has felt welcome on the highway. There were discouraging times, there were bad times—in everyone's experience. It's a road with many physical and sometimes invisible twists and turns.

Sometimes I believe we tend to romanticize that period—we, living today, who weren't there to experience it. This road became, as Steinbeck called it in *The Grapes of Wrath*, "the Mother Road." It was a nurturing road, but not everyone on the road, and not every place, was a nurturing stop.

Many of Route 66's incarnations—through the Depression, through the Great War, through World War II, and through the heyday years after the war—were times when this country was racially divided. Right up into the mid-1960s and even beyond.

So it would have been very difficult for an African American family traveling Route 66. (Not only Route 66, of course, but anywhere in the country, certainly through the mid-South or the Deep South.) Would they find a place to stay for the night, or a place to get a hot meal, or gasoline, or a restroom, or just a drink of water? That would have been very difficult on Route 66 as elsewhere.

But the irony is that road has always been itself a road of color. A road of all sorts of ethnic groups, a rainbow road.

So to me, Route 66 is a linear village that runs from Chicago to Santa Monica through these eight states. And along the way you have various neighborhoods in this village. Some are tranquil as a country graveyard; some are rough-and-tumble. Some are Italian, some black. Some are redneck, some blueblood. Some are a mix of both.

At the beginning, there was a tremendous demand and the timing was right for these automobiles. They became affordable to the everyman and everywoman. They were no longer just the play toy of the wealthy and affluent. Now, a schoolteacher could have an automobile. Now a draftsman could drive a car, or a farmer could drive a car. A clerk and a businessperson could have a car.

And with the swell of interest in cars, the Good Roads Movement was already building, and we simply needed these highways. And when it happened, and when it was born officially, November of 1926, the road was an immediate success. Cyrus Avery (who guided 66 to Oklahoma), being the visionary that he was, sensed that. And all of these, largely men, from these various states met and forged this highway system and this highway idea. And tried to accommodate this flow of traffic. It connected two-thirds of the continent.

There were other roads before it, you know. We talk always about the old Lincoln Highway and the predecessors of Route 66, the Ozark Trail and so forth. But this highway! Those double sixes rolled off the tongue and, I think, just seemed to strike a cord with the American public.

What I like about Route 66 and—what I don't get when I'm on the turnpike or on the superslab—is the old road puts you right into the ecology of the land. I'm right there, next to the bar ditch, and I can smell that freshly cut clover. I can smell those fertile fields. I can see the farmer's wife in her pink rollers out on the plow. I can smell the hogs. I can smell the roadkill.

I actually can hear the poetry in that road, up in the land of Lincoln. Beginning right there, all the way out to Santa Monica. The tattoo of the eighteen-wheelers. The poetry of all the people who came down this road. The legions of travelers and tourists, the Okies, the disenfranchised, and so forth.

Today on the road, we have Road Warriors. They could be from Geneva, they could be from Japan. They could be twenty-five years old, or nineteen years old, or ninety years old. They could be African American or German. Some of them are yuppies, and some of them are blue-haired ladies in Airstream trailers. And some of them are tycoons, and some of them are tramps. Some of them are old hippies. It's a potpourri; it's like a rich chile stew. They cut across demographics and everything else. The one thing that they all have in common is this tremendous zeal and passion—sometimes to the point of being fanatical—for Route 66.

There's nothing wrong with most of that fanaticism. There are a lot of worse things people could do with their time.

KICKING 66

ROBERT M. DAVIS

— 1995 —

Robert Murray Davis is the road's Antichrist. Someone had to take on this ever-burgeoning myth of Route 66, he told himself at one point, and why not an English professor from Oklahoma, the state with the longest stretch of Route 66?

This excerpt is from an interview conducted in Edmond, Oklahoma, the town for which Edmond Threatt was named. In its early days it served as a Route 66 stopping point with well-known cafés. Davis is a well-read professor and a professional curmudgeon who decided not to believe the happy hype of Route 66. His remarks constitute an alternative view of this most famous road, as he reminds us of its aura of disuse and decay, of the many people who broke down or were swindled there, of the hard traveling and sad times. There is a place in the burgeoning Route 66 industry for The Man Tired of Route 66: Route 66 was a place with a lot of bad food, lumpy mattresses, and bad attitudes toward strangers. Time has winnowed those memories for many, but not for Davis.

Robert Murray Davis retired from the University of Oklahoma, having written and edited nearly two dozen scholarly volumes, plus poetry and a memoir. His article "Kicking 66" appeared in the Cimarron Review *in July 1996. His recent work is on contemporary culture:* Playing Cowboys: Low Culture and High Art *(1994) and* Mid-Life Mojo: A Guide for the Newly Single Male *(2003).*

I was born in Lyons, Kansas, in the Dust Bowl. My father was about the same age as Tom Joad, if Tom Joad had been real. My family moved around all over southern Kansas and ultimately to Missouri, where I grew up.

My first experience with Route 66 was on a trip to Albuquerque to visit relatives with my mother. We stopped at 66 west of El Reno. Then it was all Route 66—no interstates at that time. That would have been in 1952.

We were driving at night across the Texas Panhandle, and I kept wanting to pass this car and I saw this light coming. It came and came and never did come and finally a train went past on the railroad, and now those tracks have been torn up. I had never been any place that flat before.

I'm not sure Route 66 does any great harm: this touristy, retro taste. But it hasn't got anything to do with history or reality. Probably the most realistic literary depiction of Route 66 is Steinbeck's *The Grapes of Wrath*. He actually knew about Route 66—but he didn't know anything about Highway 62 from Sallisaw to Oklahoma City—he'd never been there. He gets the color of the dirt wrong, the topography wrong, and everything else wrong.

The publicity, or hype, of Route 66 has affected all of our imaginations. When I came back from a trip to California, I was talking about writing a piece [against Route 66]. I was in a cafeteria with three professors. The civil engineer said, "Hey, it was better than what came before!" The architect into historic preservation said, "You get to go through all those marvelous towns!" Another said, "See me later: I've some tales to tell."

Route 66 was a dangerous road, all these old cars broke down. And hot! I remember crossing the Mojave Desert behind campers pulling boats on two-lane roads with no air-conditioning at 112 degrees. It just about seemed to me hell.

Zooming across at seventy-five miles per hour on an interstate—that I regarded as much more superior. I see just as much, probably more, than a driver would have on Old 66.

People got ripped off. Then the fake Indian jewelry, with the series of signs that would get them, if not arrested, at least seriously reprimanded now for the kind of racist language. A guy from San Diego said the biggest problem driving Route 66 was explaining to a kid who just spent his allowance on a tomahawk that Taiwan was an Indian village.

The Route 66 phenomenon, it's older people and Europeans. Most of Route 66 is pretty boring—until you get within sight of the mountains in New Mexico and then forty to fifty miles on the other side of Flagstaff—other than that, what's to see? There are no towns worth stopping in. There's no culture with a capital "C." There is no original "there" there on Route 66. It's all an MGM pharaoh's temple. You've seen some of the surviving vernacular architecture pieces, and if you blow those up two hundred and fifty times you get a Las Vegas casino! It also proves that P. T. Barnum is right, there's a lot of suckers in the world.

ON ROUTE 66 IN TEXAS

DELBERT TREW

– 1940s –

Delbert Trew grew up on ranches along Route 66 near Glenrio, and now lives outside Alanreed, Texas. Many Route 66 travelers, following an old alignment, end up in his front yard. You'd know it if you passed his place: there's barbed wire twisted into fantastic shapes. Delbert and his wife, Ruth, run the Devil's Rope Museum in McLean, a museum dedicated to barbed wire. Inside, the traveler finds tiny dioramas of copper-colored wire, which Trew has twisted into scenes of Texas life. Alongside this is the Route 66 Museum of Texas, where one walks into a re-created Route 66 diner so authentic you can smell the grease on the menus.

Trew is one of the founders of the Texas Route 66 Association and a historical columnist for the Amarillo Globe-News. *To say that he's dedicated to preserving Route 66 in Texas is just to hint at the depth of his commitment.*

Delbert Trew is the author of works on Texas history, including Notes and Tales on Texas's Old Route 66 *(1990) and* Here and Gone *(2002).*

What happened to 66 is it just evolved out. It was time. Progress just took its toll, though it was terrible that they shut it down. Everywhere Route 66 was bypassed the town just became a ghost town. But if you look back now in retrospect, for every ghost town it created, it created cities and good towns, progressive towns.

The people who actually built the cement part of Route 66, the concrete with the thumpety-thumpety-thumpety-thump ridges in it, those people were unemployed, out of work, from every walk of life at the bottom of the Depression. They had nothing. They just walked along with the crews and worked where they could. And when they didn't have a job, they sat and waited until a job showed up. Hopefully the next day. They slept on the ground on cardboard and under canvas, just like our homeless people do today. But one fellow told me that he followed Route 66 for one hundred and fifty miles, working nearly every day.

See, many people considered California a better place to go than heaven. Because you had to die to go to heaven, but all you had to do to get to California was either hitchhike or walk or just load up and go.

In the beginning of Route 66, there was no gasoline tax. And the gasoline tax is really the only travel tax there is, because only the people who travel the roads pay the tax. The government knew they needed a road and they didn't have the money to do it, so they authorized a road and it was built. This was before highway departments, this was before right-of-way departments, this was before the right of eminent domain [was used], where they could take right-of-way, take land, and build it for the good of the people. There were no statistics on tourism, on how to build roads, how to make them hold up. None of this was in place. Route 66 brought all of that about. That is the really important part that I believe Route 66 played.

The road becomes more busy, more busy, more busy, more busy. The government says, "Hey, we got to do something. These states and these poor counties, these people can't do this alone. Their tax base won't stand this."

So that's when they come up with the taxes on gasoline. They decided to send it to the government and let it allot it out where it was needed. So, starting in the 1920s, this is where all of our big highway system begins.

In the very beginning, when Route 66 was authorized, there actually was no one around to build it. There was no equipment to run a string of cement 2,400 miles long. You had a lot of payoffs and bribery. Over in Oklahoma and even here in Texas, if you wanted a piece of the action about all you had to do was go talk to the commissioners or go talk to somebody and you could get 66 to come by your house.

Another thing were the wrecks. We very seldom had wrecks until all of the sudden we got a lot of traffic, and they were moving fast and a lot of them were traveling twenty-four hours a day.

Let's use Bonnie and Clyde as an example. Bonnie and Clyde loved Route 66 because they could move fast. We have the same thing today. Almost every day we have a drug bust here in our area. Route 66, or the interstate, is not only a road for the good people; it was also a quick road for the bad people.

We're cowboys or ranchers, always have been, and one day we drove up to the Texaco station here to have a flat fixed on the pickup. And out of a car stepped this man with shorts on! Flowers and things on them. Me and the other cowboy we thought he'd forgot his pants, we thought he'd climbed out of his car without his trousers on. He got very upset at us 'cause we were pointing and laughing at his shorts, but that was showing you the time change.

After the war, the traffic got much younger. Up until then most of the traffic was older people, 'cause they was the ones that had the money and the cars. But immediately after World War II was over, and the boys came home, then of course business picked up. It was very profitable there for a while, and a lot of people had cars and these people were used to traveling, and so the traffic became faster and thicker. The stores had more traffic through them, the gas stations: tremendous business.

The people going north and south had money in their pocket, they had cars and they were traveling from hotel to motel to various resorts. But not so on Route 66. Everybody was broke, everybody was on hard dime, they were driving old wrecks, and they were just barely making it from place to place. A lot of them were traveling from relative to relative.

Mostly it was people changing jobs. Route 66 has always been known as the road of flight. They were fleeing from one time to hopefully better times. Route 66 offered the greatest promise of any alternative that they had.

Today, about the only people we get on Route 66 now are what we call our "Route 66 nuts," cruisers. People who are really searching for Route 66. I have a suspicion they are also searching for an older time in life or maybe a little better time. We have older travelers who travel trying to see if Route 66 is really as tough as Grandma or Grandpa said it was.

Nostalgia probably contributes to the travel. But if you're really looking at your pennies traveling, all you've got to do is get off the interstate a few blocks and your motel will go down ten to twenty bucks a night. You food will go from eight to ten dollars down to six bucks. Gas will often drop ten cents. That is merely pulling off the highway. That has some followers. (And of course we have the people like you folks, writing and interviewing.)

They're tired of plastic. I think they're tired of TV. I think that they are tired of reading cruddy books with all the porn—they want to get away on old Route 66. Because they have somewhere to go and they can't stray too far.

We have a little over eighteen thousand vehicles every twenty-four hours travel the interstate. Now over 50 percent of those are big trucks. And so we have some people who say, "Man, I've had about all of this

I can take for today. I'm going to get off on the edge awhile." So you just move over a block or get over on the surface road, you can slow down, you can roll your window down, and you can stop if you want to take a photo.

My prediction is that sometime in the future what is Interstate 40 will be strictly for trucks. You'll have to weigh eight thousand pounds to even get on them. And then to either side of that will be where cars drive, smaller vehicles, and they're going to be traveling old Route 66.

People who live on Route 66 take it for granted. Maybe we travel it everyday. I did this for a while in the beginning until I began to get interested and involved with the museums and writing about it.

I live at the Jericho Gap. Typical politicians: they didn't give us any money. The larger cities and larger counties had some money and they could do better. But when you get to Alanreed, Texas, there was only

four ranches in next fifty miles of road. You couldn't expect those four ranches to pay enough taxes to pave the road. There were sections of road that were not paved, not gravel, just not improved at all. And one of these was the Jericho Gap. What made it really bad was that it was sticky-gumbo mud. If it'd been gravel or sandy land it would have been better. But it was the blackest stickiest old gumbo you ever saw. Miles of it. But there was a good side. A lot of farmers made a livin' pulling those people out of the mud holes.

If you'd been here four or five years ago we had a couple waltz across Texas . . . and walking is easier than waltzing. The neat thing about it was the man couldn't dance backwards, so the lady he danced with had to dance backwards. So she waltzed across Texas backwards. One hundred and seventy-eight miles.

Steinbeck called it the "Mother Road," and you've got to think about that a little bit. America fled west to new country, the new world out there. And the "Mother Road" nourished them all of the way. No matter how broke, no matter how bad your old truck was, no matter what kind of problems you had, somehow or other you made it out there. Do you know of any other highway anywhere that has this sort of thing said about it?

Shamrock, Texas

CADILLAC RANCH

STANLEY MARSH III

— 1970s —

Mention the name Stanley Marsh in Amarillo, Texas, and you're bound
to get a shake of the head and a chuckle. "A character!" they'll tell you.
This is the story of a man inspired to take ten Cadillacs of varying years
and bury them headfirst in the Texas plain. Although it's the most famous artwork on Route 66, it never was on Route 66, and never will be;
it sits on I-40 as it bypasses 66. His idea, and the Ant Farm (the artists
who actually carried it out), have been featured in a Bruce Springsteen
song and in countless photo essays. Periodically the Cadillacs are painted
white to get rid of the graffiti—which begins again the next day.

Stanley Marsh was raised rich, Texas-style. His maids had Cadillacs
when he was growing up, he said. Though part owner of a chain of television stations and deeply invested in energy corporations, Stanley Marsh
considers himself an iconoclast. Cadillac Ranch is the most famous of his
creations, but he has more such installations on a ranch outside of Amarillo. In this interview, he works hard to portray himself as an eccentric.
Instead he seems tired, racist, and arrogant. Despite all of this, in Cadillac Ranch he has created a moving monument to mobility, Texas-style. As
those Cadillacs pitch into the ground, they are a static monument to the
dreams of many driving Route 66.

Cadillacs. Imagine those turquoise Cadillacs and the titty-pink ones. They were something, but people thought they were beautiful. The majority of people in this country, they lived on the East Coast. They wanted to hit the road and go to Las Vegas and break the bank and go to Hollywood and go to the beach and find a blonde and then they wanted to be a movie star and that was the American Dream . . .

We won the war and it was our right to have those big cars and we had the gas right here in Texas and we had the right to be optimistic and want to break the bank in Las Vegas and be movie stars. Cadillac Ranch—it's a monument. It's a stepping-stone. It was the reason that the Americans became optimistic and we can believe in superheroes today. We can believe in the American mono-myth.

I was born right here in Amarillo, Texas. January 31, 1938. My momma was a little redheaded girl from Oklahoma and my daddy was good looking. He was going to be in the natural gas business. And he was buying natural gas. My ancestors had come out here because of transportation; this was the nearest place with roads and railroads and telegraph.

When I was growing up, I didn't realize that Highway 66 was significant. I just thought it was the big road out there. And I didn't know until its birthday a couple of years ago that it only went from Chicago to L.A. . . . And I wrote a ninth grade paper about tourism as Amarillo's industry. But it was the tourism of the truck stop. I called around and I think it was our third-biggest industry. At the time you rode the train or you drove on Highway 66. The cars would go about two hundred and fifty miles a day. They were unreliable so you'd spend the night in Oklahoma City, spend the night in Amarillo, spend the night in Albuquerque. And filling stations and motels and eateries and that sort of thing employed more people and provided more jobs in the town of Amarillo in 1950, when we had seventy thousand.

I had seen a book called *The History of the Cadillac Tail Fins*, so I knew what they were shaped like and I did what any normal person would do when I saw the book: I folded out the page with the tail fins and I tore it off and stole it out of the Amarillo library and stuffed it in my tunic.

I always thought it was 66 after Phillips 66 and I still to this day believe it was 69 at the first and the Baptists went out at night and sawed it off and just turned them around so it wouldn't be so offensive to them. So it's really 69. I know, I was there. I saw it. I'm a witness to it.

This is not the road to California. I don't want to go out there with those squishy head, orange-juice-drinking fairies. Not on your life. This is the road to the East Coast. To our pilgrims' fathers and England where I belong, except they've been letting so many foreigners in England, it's not even all white anymore. This is the road to Buckingham Palace. I don't live on a road to Los Angeles. I live in Amarillo, Texas. I am Amarillo, Texas. Amarillo, Texas, would dry up and blow away if I weren't here. If I woke up dead they simply would burn down the town and abandon it and there would be a big volcano here, that's all there would be.

It's weird. I was out talking to [Route 66] the other day and I said, "You're old and you're flat and you just go every place straight and look at me, there has been so much of me now. I've finally gotten to be as big as Moby Dick. And I can dance like Moby Dick and you're just as straight and as boring as Captain Ahab's old wooden leg, flopping up and down on Moby Dick's back." And [Route 66] just rolled all up around me like a piece of licorice pretending it was a cobra snake and it rolled all around itself.

I spit in its eye. And it spit back in mine.

"Lie down," I said. "Lie down on the ground where you belong. A road should be a road or I'll make you into a graveyard or a waterfall and you will fall into the ground. You could be Niagara Falls or you could be Highway 66, but not both. Take your choice."

You think I am making a mock of you. That I am making short of what you are doing. That I am using you or something like that because I am not being factual and not sounding like the encyclopedia. I am demonstrating to you the absolute power and glory that comes with owning a national treasure. I own the only national treasure that has ever been suggested to be put on a coin, a stamp, or a dollar bill. And that is power, baby. So I can say anything about it I want to. I am unrestrained by the normal courtesies of life.

To my way of thinking, the biggest challenge facing an artist in the United States, the biggest challenge facing the sculptor anyplace, is a flat horizon line. An absolutely flat horizon line. That is a challenge, baby. That's all there is to it. It's easy to enough to deal with hills and

valleys and oceans or riverbeds or mine holes or whatever you have, but when you have the endless prairie, a horizon line as far as you can see, and the sun above, and not one feature on it, anything you put on it is going to seem alien.

But to describe what Cadillac Ranch looks like, what the horizon looks like, what a hawk circling in the evening looks like . . . You can only expect one or two good artists to be alive and working at any given time in the Western world, and I am one of them.

MOUNTAIN 66
NEW MEXICO AND ARIZONA

Between Kingman and Oatman, Arizona

MINING ALONG 66

RAYMOND WIERTH AND JOE MILLER

— 1920s —

Route 66's early days marked a transition from stagecoaches and freight wagons to cars. This transitional era is difficult to imagine today, and the reader is lucky to have these interviews recorded in 1980 with two gents who mined on Route 66 at the border of Arizona and California. This oral history is from those who dug and hauled and prospected hard-rock mining in the West. Theirs was an often lonely life.

This is hard-rock Route 66, the Mother Road as the Mother Lode. Picking their way into the night, these miners looked down from their desert mountains and watched changes in the fragile, isolated West. It's the story of wagon ruts paved for not only the newfangled Model T, but also for mining trucks. The West offered sustenance to such people, but not much. Often, the well was dry from previous travelers.

This is Route 66 at its most sinuous, as it crosses Oatman in the Black Mountains at Sitgreaves Pass. The road mounts up to the mines and turns sharply through a hundred curves between the Colorado and this range. No guardrails or lights, with drops of hundreds of feet below. At night, wild burros sometimes stop cars on the road.

Here are two lives on 66, lived in crevices in the stony hills separating California and Arizona. They are presented laconically, in the western style: simple tales of men who led difficult lives that never strayed far from the Mother Road. They are excerpted from the extensive oral history collection of the Mohave County archives, in Kingman, Arizona.

RAYMOND WIERTH:

I was born in New Bremen, Ohio, on April 22, 1897. I first came to Kingman in 1922.

I had read about gold mining in Oatman: that's one reason I came to this area. I didn't get to Oatman, I stayed in Kingman. I mined in the Hualapai Mountains, worked my own claim, mostly for silver. When I was mining I would ship the ore out raw, right to the smelters. They smelted it for me and paid me for it. Maybe once a week or once a month I would come into town for supplies. I spent the winters there in the early '30s, working the claims, and for a couple of years I lived underground. I dug a tunnel and my sleeping quarters were in another part. At night when I went to bed the bats would be flying around, which never bothered me. There would be some mice crawling around the bed. They never bothered me either.

I had no wife. The mining that I did paid a living at that time. Living by myself, it didn't cost very much. I never married. When World War II started I had to quit mining, because they wouldn't let me. Then I joined the Army Air Corps. I was in there from 1942 to 1943. I was let out because of my age. I was already forty-six years old when I got in. During the war years, I worked at the air base as a stationary engineer. In the beginning I helped build [the base] and that's where I finished the war years.

There was one road that went to California, and it was called the Old Trails Road, which is now Highway 66. It went south on Fourth Street until where Walter's Cycle Shop is; it turns to the right and a little bit to the left again to the railroad tracks. We followed the railroad tracks until we got to where the California inspection station was. Then we crossed the railroad tracks to the other side of the Colorado River [Arizona], and went to Oatman. Route 66 went to Oatman, unpaved, and then to Topock and then to Needles. Needles was seventy-two miles from Kingman at that time. The road to Yucca was not much more than a trail. And the road leading the other way to the Hualapais went through Slaughter House Canyon. That was the only way to get there.

It was pretty rough going, the highway was.

JOE MILLER:

I was born in Hackberry [Arizona] in 1899, on August 9. My parents had lived a good many years down on the Sandy River near Hackberry before I was born. They were pioneers, raising cattle, and moved to Hackberry in the early '90s. At that time, Hackberry was the main town in the county, shipping cattle on the railroad. I don't know when the railroad came through, but it was through then. There were Indians (Hualapai and others) around then, working on the ranches. The government issued them flour and sugar, even beef.

My mother and father both died and my uncle, George Keiser, and his brother Frank came and got us kids and brought us to Kingman. I went to school a little before that, but when we came to Kingman I started to go to school here in 1910 in the little brick library building, the little red schoolhouse, and graduated from the eighth grade there in 1916.

There wasn't hardly anything here in those days. I remember we arrived in Kingman in the middle of the night by train, and we went to the Beale Hotel, which at that time was just the front old section and it had a porch built out over the sidewalk, torn off now. From the second floor, you could walk out above the porch [over Route 66] and look around. That first morning I came out and saw the actor Andy Devine riding burros around here. Burros were just roaming the streets then, not wild, but just left over from prospectors, kind of like in Oatman. There was a law that you couldn't keep them tied up unless you fed them hay, and us kids didn't have hay so we had to turn them loose. The next day there was a rush to see who got the burros; the person who got 'em got to have 'em for the day. There was one or two of 'em would buck a little, but most of them were just gentle.

We made our own entertainment. There weren't no ballgames or nothing at that time. There wasn't even any automobiles. They started to come in about that time. The mines were running, and the county was booming pretty good. The stage lines to Chloride and Oatman and Gold Road were all horse and buggy. I remember the old freight wagons pulling out of here, loaded, up Stockton Hill. At that time the road went up here by the white cliffs where Route 66 runs. The old freight wagons wore that train [of ruts] in the tufa stone.

A freight wagon would have all the way from twelve to twenty horses and they weren't very big wagons either. Today our small trucks haul as much as those big wagons.

Oatman, Arizona

HOT SATURDAY

HARVEY FERGUSSON

– 1926 –

----

*When miners and ranchers came to town on a Saturday night, riding into
the big city, they wanted a high time. Albuquerque was known for this
and for the "wool wagons" rolling into town covered with hides and wool
from the distant reservations. At the dawn of Route 66, Albuquerque was
becoming a social and economic center along U.S. 66, with now-classic
auto courts. This next excerpt brings us there, with a Whitman-esque
evocation of fun on the frontier in the 1920s.*

*This cameo of the largest city between St. Louis and Los Angeles—
Albuquerque—captures the duality of its geography: tall mountains and a
high plain, where once the Big River (Rio Grande) stretched a mile wide.*

*Though Albuquerque is today cosmopolitan, with a metro area near-
ing three-quarters of a million, the city and its isolated state are two
hundred and fifty miles from the nearest metropolitan center. "Poor New
Mexico," a popular saying goes, "so far from God, and so near Texas."
Route 66's stretch across New Mexico was its last section paved, in 1937.
Eleven years earlier, as this story takes place, a hot Saturday in the high
desert offered saloons and bars, exotic dances, and fiestas. All this, out on
the rough traces of Route 66, where prohibition is unknown and cars are
the new parlor.*

*Harvey Fergusson and his sister Erna were among the first popular
novelists to write with authenticity about the mix of cultures of New
Mexico. An Albuquerque native and author of a dozen books on the*

Southwest, Fergusson's work has been adapted for film, including Stand
Up and Fight *(1939) and* Hot Saturday *(1932), which starred Cary Grant.*

Mountains that had been mystery and danger to one generation
were a toy to the next. Pioneers had approached mountains with
prayer, tightening their belts for want and effort, and their children
flew up them and over them, spooned and feasted on their austere
heights, found nothing there to harden body or spirit. . . . Mountains
were no longer barriers nor adventure . . .

To-night the town will dance at seven public dances of assorted
grade, from the one in Dogtown where sheep-herders and mechanics,
cowboys and brakemen, greaser and gringo, hunk and wop, will meet,
get full of corn, and fight with brass knucks, quirts, monkey wrenches
and pocket knives over soft-eyed girls from Old Town, to the one at
Willow Springs where sons and daughters of first families will neck and
drink discreetly in limousines between fox-trots. No one will lack a girl
if he has a dollar and sticks to his own gang.

To-night the town will drink and everyone who wants shall have
his liquor. At the Center Street Barber Shop he can get what looks
and tastes like pre-war Scotch, but isn't, for ten dollars a quart, and at
the Crossroads Garage he can get white mule and native grape brandy
for half the price, and it will lift him just as high and let him down
no harder.

To-night the town will gamble. Fifty poker games are starting now
and they range from penny-ante, with wives sitting in, to the stern and
silent all-night contest with a ten-dollar limit in a back room at the
Elks Club. Behind a locked door over the Gold Star pool-room a crap
game rattles and clinks, curses and prays in a circle of sweating faces
round a pile of silver and bills. . . . Elderly bridge addicts glare at each
other across the dummy in homes deserted by the young.

To-night the town will make love. It has a thousand dates. Soon after dark it will throw off flying cars in all directions, like yellow sparks
from a pin-wheel, all seeking to bury themselves in the purple night,
looking for dark quiet places to park with lights out and curtains drawn.

Cars are privacy and escape. Cars run away from home and mother,
wife and neighbour, make the world fifty miles wider and easier to

hide in. Cars carry young lovers, bathed and powdered, with eager lips and curious fingers, stealthy married men with cuties cuddled beside them, young bucks with shopgirls and waitresses swiftly picked up on Second Street. . . . Cars loaded with desire vanish as points of burning red into the purple night.

Albuquerque

THE THIN MOUNTAIN AIR

PAUL HORGAN

– 1930s –

If cars were all the rage for the Jazz Age visitor to the mountain West, by the '30s, bicycles also had their place on 66 among the young, the poor, and the young at heart. This next piece reminds us of all the great conversations one can have on a bike.

What always distinguished New Mexico's Route 66 is what distinguishes the state itself: it was the first in fifty to have a majority of its citizens from minority groups. Here, newly arrived gringos—called Anglos—drive up in their new shiny sedans and stare at the bent viejitos *in their '50 Chevy trucks. Along 66 they gaze into the eyes of the Other, and the Other looks back.*

Paul Horgan was a versatile author on the Southwest, publishing short stories, novels, children's books, poems, plays, even a libretto. His half-dozen novels explore the multicultural character of New Mexico and the Southwest, particularly the Mountain Standard Time *trilogy:* Main Line West *(1936),* Far From Cibola *(1938), and* The Common Heart *(1942). His history of the Rio Grande and biography,* Lamy of Santa Fe *(1975), won a Pulitzer Prize.*

We had bought a Ford Touring car, black, like all the Fords, in which Sam or I or Lillian (who learned to drive with the same reckless competence with which she attacked the typewriter) drove my mother on her errands and visits. For myself, they had given me a new bicycle, an Indian Flier, which gave me independence in my explorations of the city, the great empty plain of the mesa between town and mountain, and the Rio Grande. Lillian bought me a klaxon horn for my handlebars "for safety" and I demonstrated the sound for her— "oo-ah, oo-ah."

There were three parts to the town. The central part was built in a grid about the Santa Fe tracks, and in fact, the main street was called Central Avenue [Route 66], which cut across the tracks at right angles. In its middle section, for several blocks, the main commerce of the town went on in shops, movie theaters, offices. Above, to the east, rose the residential town into the sand hills which led to the mesa, at whose edge the university marked the city limits.

Ten miles away, in a grand arched profile, lay the Sandia Mountains, pale rocky-brown by day, with blue clefts and inky cloud shadows over their many faces. To their south, another range, the Manzanos, dwindled away in fading blue ridges. At evening, the mountains were washed by a deep rose glow, and at night, during the full moons, they abided in a sort of silvery dark wall against the pale moonlit sky. The other end of town, to the West, reached from the twentieth century into the eighteenth when Central Avenue arrived at the original settlement beside the Rio Grande—(Old Town).

I rode everywhere to see the town and watch the people. As everyone discovered, there were three distinct orders of people—the Indians who came into town from their pueblos to sell their pottery and weavings; the Latin descendants of the first conquerors; and the Anglo-Americans, like us, who represented the third occupation of the land, and now dominated it, in all material ways . . .

"It will be a long time before they will be allowed to join it," said Lyle when we were talking about the laminated society one evening.

"But why?" I asked. "They were here before us. They even have the very look of the land."

"True, true, kid, but it's all a matter of who has the power, meaning the money and the know-how. You know who. You, your father, me, the Anglo bankers, railroaders, doctors. And like all colonists, we bring our style of life with us, and we make it prevail over the old life we find here, and the two don't yet mix, or if they do at all, they mix on our terms."

"Sam says they resent us—he has read all he could get about the

Southwest, and he says it goes way back to the Mexican War and the American conquest."

"Don't you feel it?"

"No, the Mexicans I run into are polite."

"Spoken like a true colonist. The natives know their place: how convenient: and they damn well better, y'know?—Isn't that the usual attitude?"

"I suppose it is."

"Well, let me suggest that you avoid getting caught alone in Old Town, or up in the sand hills, if there's a gang of Mexican kids around. You and your nice shiny red Indian Flier bike . . ."

"They won't bother me."

"Don't give them a chance."

"I don't feel hostile. Why should they?"

"You don't have any reason to. They do."

"But why?"

"Have you ever been an underdog in your own back yard?—See how you'd like it."

LAGUNA EXILE

MARY TOYA

— 1930s —

Those crossing New Mexico by car found little water and too much sun. Since the coming of the Spaniards in the seventeenth century, expeditions across the Southwest (New Spain) have always had the ironic effect of making second-class citizens of those who lived here. Privilege has gone to the traveler. The Bible says, "The first ones now shall later be last," and this adage reflects the fate of the descendants of the ancianos of this continent. Spaniards suppressed and enslaved Indians; Anglos bullied their way over Hispanic and Indian both.

In the Southwest, the span of time is long. Where in the East, five generations of family is enough to make you Back Bay respectable. Out West five generations is the lifetime of an adobe wall, and walls crumble to dust in the twinkle of history's eye.

Because of Route 66, the Laguna Pueblo in New Mexico had plenty of tourists. In varying pavements, the Old Road has run through its main street for eighty-five years. For the Laguna in Winslow, Arizona—mainly railroad workers—life was harder, yet as rich as their Pueblo. Their residence, Indian Camp, is today a deserted triangle of weeds between the rails and what was U.S. Highway 66. In this field are rusting pieces of the old boxcar Mary Toya first called home and later called a prison.

Mary Toya is the daughter of Helen Andrea Toya, one of the original generation of Laguna railroad workers who lived in Winslow's "Box Car Village." Her father painted locomotives. The family was actively involved in tribal activities, including Winslow baseball and musical bands.

I was born in a boxcar so I don't have a birth certificate. I go by my baptismal certificate for my date of birth.

I guess my mother got pregnant, and she sat down with her babies in a boxcar because actually the Indian Health Hospital was a hospital for tuberculosis patients only. The railroad did not provide my father with any hospital insurance or anything for the small hospital they had there. My father lived somewhere close to Santa Fe Railroad yard.

The railroad needed workers to come out here, and they needed that land to put their tracks through the reservation. That would connect to the West Coast. If they had detoured around Laguna, it would have taken more miles to lay the tracks. So, in exchange for the land that the railroad tracks went through, they promised jobs to Laguna people.

I remember going to Mesita [on the Laguna Pueblo] on the weekends. We'd leave [Winslow, Arizona] after my father got off work late Friday, and we'd arrive at Mesita [New Mexico] probably around midnight because you couldn't go seventy miles per hour in a car packed full of kids. The speed limit was about fifty or fifty-five miles an hour then so it used to take us forever to get to Mesita. So, when we'd hit the dirt road off old Route 66 to go up to the village, we knew we were at Mesita and everybody woke up. We were just really happy my Grandma and Grandpa would be waiting for us even if it was after midnight. They had their kerosene lamp going.

Route 66 was just a road to town, just another highway. We didn't realize it was going to be in history books. At that time when we were growing up and going to school, we just walked off on Route 66 to go to the high school. People from the East Coast thought it was kind of strange to see all these Indian people walking around in regular street clothes, not wearing any tomahawks or feathers in their hair and moccasins—you know, the stereotype Hollywood has created. There were a lot of Indian people that lived in Winslow at that time, Hopis and Navajos and Lagunas and some other pueblos came.

Our people were willing to work hard, earn a living. Maybe they were less affected by the heat—I think that had a lot to do with it. They were big men, strong and husky men. My dad, he was about 5'8", very broad shoulders, and very, very strong. I think that that had a lot to do with hiring a lot of Indian people.

When I was a child, we more or less couldn't leave our little compound on the Indian Camp. Unless we were with our parents. As we started growing up, my mom and dad used to drop us off at the movie theater and then pick us up later; or he'd have to tell them at the theater that he was going to have us walk back to the Indian Camp. Years later, as I grew up and left Winslow, I felt that we were almost held like prisoners at the Indian Camp. They had a wooden fence around, and they had big gates. And then a little further from where the Indian Camp ended and the "Jap" quarters started—where the Japanese people used to live—they had a chain link fence where you could go through, for the people to walk through a little gate.

They'd lock that at night so you couldn't go out; and you weren't allowed to go through the big gate where the cars and trucks came in to go to work.

When I grew up, and the more I realized how it was, I felt like we were held prisoners there. After dark we really couldn't go anywhere, into town or anything.

It was like a little Indian reservation, and we had our own governor and people, and they'd always told us to behave, and you know, told us to be courteous and be polite, and don't get into fights.

Indian Camp was just a whole bunch of rows of boxcars, six on the south side and six on the north side. They gave you the amount of boxcars you needed because of your family, so we had two together. And one of them, it was the upper one, was just one huge long bedroom. My dad put a partition: one was their room and the other part was the kids' room. My mother and father had us sleeping in the crib until I was about five years old, and it was embarrassing.

In the other boxcar was my mother's kitchen, living room, dining room. And then my dad put another partition with a door to keep the cold air out, and that's where my mother had her woodbin. We had to keep that filled. As I got older, that was my job, to keep the wood box full for our potbelly stove and her cooking stove. Winslow's at about 4,900 feet above sea level. In winter, it was very, very cold. But those boxcars, they were very warm.

In school, after about a year of sitting on the floor eating our lunch, we finally got to sit at tables, but we had to wait until all the white kids got through eating before we could sit down and eat. They even served us sour milk, but my dad went up there with friends and we never had sour milk after that.

The Japanese lived just a ditch away, working on the railroad. Then they took 'em off during the Second World War. That was really sad. We were having one of our religious ceremonies [in the kiva made from two boxcars], when I saw the army herding them out. They came in with their canvas trucks and just loaded them up. Just took 'em off. They were just treated like a bunch of cattle, and those people never did anything to anybody. They were just real nice people.

At Laguna Mart last year, I was going into the store and some Route 66 tourists asked me where they were.

"You're in Laguna Pueblo," I said.

"Well, where's the reservation?" they said.

"You're standing on the reservation," I said.

"Well, where are the teepees?" they asked.

"What teepees?" I said.

"Well, this tourist guide book said we could see some teepees."

"You have the wrong reservation. You need to go back several thousand miles and go to Plains Indians," I said. "They're the ones with the teepees. We have adobe or rock houses. See those up there, that's houses."

"Well, the tourist guide book said we were gonna find teepees."

"Well, you don't find teepees around here," I said.

"How can we get back on Route 66?" they said.

There was another person going into the store from my village and he was talking to me in Keresan, my language.

"How come you don't just tell 'em if they keep asking you questions that we're gonna take 'em over to the kiva," he said, "we're gonna spread-eagle them and we're gonna scalp 'em . . . just tell 'em anything, they'll believe it!

"If they want to find teepees, they're gonna believe anything you tell 'em anyway." He and I started laughing. They just got in their car and took off.

THE GRAPES OF WRATH

JOHN STEINBECK

– 1939 –

No writer is more responsible for drawing attention to Route 66 than John Steinbeck, who was born in California and spent his life writing of its fertile valleys and gentle coasts.

The Grapes of Wrath *had its start in a newspaper series,* The Harvest Gypsies, *which Steinbeck wrote for a San Francisco newspaper. He visited the Great Central Valley of California during the Depression and was struck by the influx of farm workers in desperation: not just Okies and Arkies, but Filipinos and Mexicans and Indians. Whether or not he actually drove the roads he describes, or, as Louis Owens will describe later in this book, sat with a map and turned 66 place names into a litany, no one really knows. In any case, John Steinbeck christened Route 66 with epithets that have stuck to this day: the Mother Road, the Old Road, the Road of Flight. When John Ford turned this great novel into film, he left America with an indelible image of Tom Joad (portrayed by Henry Fonda) scratching his head and looking west. The legend of Route 66 had begun in earnest.*

John Steinbeck wrote nearly two dozen books before revisiting 66, briefly, in Travels with Charley *(1962). That same year he won the Nobel Prize in Literature. Writing in the tradition of literary naturalism, he was never afraid to show society at its breaking point.*

H ighway 66 is the main migrant road. 66—the long concrete path across the country, waving gently up and down on the map, from the Mississippi to Bakersfield—over the red lands and the gray lands, twisting up into the mountains, crossing the Divide and down into the bright and terrible desert, and across the desert to the mountains again, and into the rich California valleys.

66 is the path of a people in flight, refugees from dust and shrinking land, from the thunder of tractors and shrinking ownership, from the desert's slow northward invasion, from the twisting winds that howl up out of Texas, from the floods that bring no richness to the land and steal what little richness is there. From all of these the people are in flight, and they come into 66 from the tributary side roads, from the wagon tracks and the rutted country roads. 66 is the mother road, the road of flight.

Clarksville and Ozark and Van Buren and Fort Smith on 64, and there's an end of Arkansas. And all the roads into Oklahoma City, 66 down from Tulsa, 270 up from McAlester. 81 from Wichita Falls south, from Enid north. Edmund, McLoud, Purcell. 66 out of Oklahoma City; El Reno and Clinton, going west on 66. Hydro, Elk City, and Texola; and there's an end to Oklahoma. 66 across the Panhandle of Texas. Shamrock and McLean, Conway and Amarillo, the yellow. Wildorado and Vega and Boise, and there's an end of Texas. Tucumcari and Santa Rosa into the New Mexican mountains to Albuquerque, where the road comes down from Santa Fe. Then down the gorged Rio Grande to Los Lunas and west again on 66 to Gallup, and there's the border of New Mexico.

And now the high mountains. Holbrook and Winslow and Flagstaff in the high mountains of Arizona. Then the great plateau rolling like a ground swell. Ashfork and Kingman and stone mountains again, where water must be hauled and sold. Then out of the broken sun-rotted mountains of Arizona to the Colorado, with green reeds on its banks, and that's the end of Arizona. There's California just over the river, and a pretty town to start it. Needles, on the river. But the river is a stranger to this place. Up from Needles and over a burned range, and there's the desert. And 66 goes on over the terrible desert, where the distance shimmers and the black center mountains hang unbearably in the distance. At last there's Barstow, and more desert until at last the mountains rise up again, the good mountains, and 66 winds through them.

Then suddenly a pass, and below the beautiful valley, below orchards and vineyards and little houses, and in the distance a city. And, oh, my God, it's over.

The people in flight streamed out on 66, sometimes a single car, sometimes a little caravan. All day they rolled slowly along the road, and at night they stopped near water. In the day ancient leaky radiators sent up columns of steam, loose connecting rods hammered and pounded. And the men driving the trucks and the overloaded cars listened apprehensively. How far between towns? It is a terror between towns. If something breaks—well, if something breaks we camp right here while Jim walks to town and gets a part and walks back and—how much food we got?

Listen to the motor. Listen to the wheels. Listen with your ears and with your hands on the steering wheel; listen with the palm of your

hand on the gear-shift lever; listen with your feet on the floor boards. Listen to the pounding old jalopy with all your senses; for a change of tone, a variation of rhythm may mean—a week here? That rattle— that's tappets. Don't hurt a bit. Tappets can rattle till Jesus comes again without no harm. But that thudding as the car moves along—can't hear that—just kind of feel it. Maybe oil isn't gettin' someplace. Maybe a bearing's startin' to go. Jesus, if it's a bearing, what'll we do? Money's goin' fast.

And why's the son-of-a-bitch heat up so hot today? This ain't no climb. Le's look. God Almighty, the fan belt's gone! Here, make a belt outa this little piece a rope. Le's see how long—there. I'll splice the ends. Now take her slow—slow, till we can get to a town. That rope belt won't last long. 'F we can on'y get to California where the oranges grow before this here ol' jug blows up. 'F we on'y can.

CEREMONY

LESLIE MARMON SILKO

– 1960s –

----

*Leslie Marmon Silko was brought up along Route 66 on the Laguna res-
ervation in New Mexico, the grandchild of Anglo and Indian ancestors.
This selection is from her extraordinary first novel. It's the story of Tayo,
a man suffering from post-traumatic stress disorder from World War II,
who tries to return along 66 to the Laguna Pueblo, where he was born.
The struggles of this character to restore balance and harmony to his life
are not met with success. Part of this is precisely due to Route 66, which
brings injustices and too many unpleasant reminders into the Pueblo and
then offers him too many easy escapes from the hard tasks that face him.
Route 66 here is a road not for Indians but for those who traffic with
them: the bar owners, the drifters who make it their temporary home.*

Silko is the author of The Turquoise Ledge *(2010),* Gardens in the
Dunes *(1999), an autobiography titled* Sacred Water *(1993),* Storyteller
(1981), Almanac of the Dead *(1991), and* Laguna Woman *(1994), a collection of verse. She received a MacArthur Fellowship in 1981 and previously taught fiction at the University of Arizona.*

"The traveling made me tired. But I remember when we drove
through Gallup. I saw Navajos in torn old jackets, standing outside
the bars. There were Zunis and Hopis there too, even a few Lagunas.
All of them slouched down against the dirty walls of the bars along
Highway 66, their eyes staring at the ground as if they had forgotten

the sun in the sky; or maybe that was the way they dreamed for wine, looking for it somewhere in the mud of the sidewalk. This is us, too, I was thinking to myself. These people crouching outside bars like cold flies stuck to the wall."

They parked the truck by the Trailways bus station and walked across the railroad tracks. It was still early in the morning, and the shadows around the warehouses and buildings were long. The streets were empty, and on a Saturday morning in Gallup, Tayo knew what they would see. From the doorway of a second-hand store he could see feet, toes poking through holes in the socks. Someone sleeping off the night before, but without his boots now, because somebody had taken them to trade for a bottle of cheap wine. The guy had his head against the door; his brown face was peaceful and he was snoring loudly. Tayo smiled. Gallup was that kind of place, interesting, even funny as long as you were just passing through, the way the white tourists did driving down 66, stopping to see the Indian souvenirs. But if you were an Indian, you attended to business and then left, and you were never in that town after dark. That was the warning the old Zunis, and Hopis, and Navajos had about Gallup. The safest way was to avoid bad places after dark.

Tee Pee Curios, Tucumcari, New Mexico

THE HITCH-HIKER

LUCILLE FLETCHER

– 1947 –

The car radio was usually the main source of entertainment on Route 66.
Many Americans first heard Spanish by tuning in to XER out of Del Rio,
Texas, where they also heard Wolfman Jack. But the radio personality
who towers above them all is Orson Welles, who starred in this taut radio
drama set on Route 66.

One of the most famous radio plays about traveling, The Hitch-Hiker
was produced in the tradition of Welles's Mercury Theatre. This eerie
tale was designed to keep the listener in Suspense—as the Announcer
used to say.

It evokes the loneliness of the long-distance traveler. Out under the
stars, alone on the two-lane highway with the last light miles behind,
a weight descends: the miles ahead, all the long days behind the wheel.
That hoped-for new personality, that new chance just around the corner
disappears every afternoon with the puddle-of-water mirages. And if the
cares of the road grow too much for the traveler—finding the next gas
pump, a decent meal not encrusted with 66 grease, or a quiet place to lay
your head—he or she will be glad there aren't other problems—such as
an elusive figure following close behind.

The Hitch-Hiker *was also produced as an episode of* The Twilight
Zone. *Another well-known suspense-thriller radio script by Lucille*
Fletcher, Sorry, Wrong Number, *was made into the 1948 film noir classic*
of the same name.

ADAMS: I am in an auto camp on Route Sixty-Six just west of Gallup, New Mexico. If I tell it, perhaps it will help me. It will keep me from going mad. But I must tell this quickly. I am not mad now. I feel perfectly well, except that I am running a slight temperature. My name is Ronald Adams. I am thirty-six years of age, unmarried, tall, dark, with a black mustache. I drive a Buick, license number 6Y-175-189. I was born in Brooklyn. All this I know. I know that I am at this moment perfectly sane. That it is not me who has gone mad—but something else—something utterly beyond my control. But I must speak quickly. At any moment the link may break. This may be the last thing I ever tell on earth . . . the last night I ever see the stars . . . (*Pause. Music fades out.*)

HITCH-HIKER: (*Off-stage, through megaphone, hollowly*) Hallooo . . . Hallo . . . ooo . . . (*MANUAL SOUND: Starter button. Sound of gears jamming. Through megaphone off-stage, closer.*) Hall-ooo . . . (*Manual sound continues. Clash of gears. Dead starter.*)

ADAMS: (*Panicky*) No—not just now. Sorry . . .

HITCH-HIKER: (*Through megaphone off-stage*) Going to Cal-I-fornia . . . a . . . ?

ADAMS: (*Panicky*) No. Not today. The other way. Going to New York. Sorry . . .

(*SOUND RECORDING: Automobile hum continuing through following.*)
After I got the car back onto the road again, I felt like a fool. Yet the thought of picking him up, of having him sit beside me was somehow unbearable. Yet at the same time, I felt more than ever, unspeakably alone . . .

Hour after hour went by. The fields, the towns, ticked off one by one. The light changed. I knew now that I was going to see him again. And though I dreaded the sight, I caught myself searching the side of the road, waiting for him to appear. . . . If I could have found a place to stop . . . to rest a little. But I was in the Ozark Mountains of Missouri now. The few resort places there were closed. Only an occasional log cabin, seemingly deserted, broke the monotony of the wild wooded landscape. . . . I knew I would see him again—perhaps at the next turn in of the road. I knew that when I saw him next— I would run him down. (*MUSIC: Dark chords, followed by eerie melody.*) But I did not see him again until late next afternoon. (*Music continues eerily. MANUAL SOUND: The tinkling of signal bell at rail-*

road crossroads. Continue through following.) I had stopped the car at a sleepy little junction just across the border into Oklahoma . . . to let a train pass by—when he appeared across the tracks, leaning against a telephone pole . . .

It was a perfectly airless, dry day. The red clay of Oklahoma was baking under the southwestern sun. Yet there were spots of fresh rain on his shoulders. . . . I couldn't stand that.

Without thinking, blindly, I started the car across the tracks. (*SOUND RECORDING: Distant, very faint cry of train whistle approaching. Manual sound of bell continuing.*) He didn't even look up at me. He was staring at the ground. I stepped on the gas hard, veering the wheel sharply toward him. (*SOUND RECORDING: Train whistle closer. Chugging of wheels fading in.*) I could hear the train in the distance now. But I didn't care. (*MANUAL SOUND ONE: Continues signal bell. MANUAL SOUND TWO: Jamming of gears. Clash of metal.*) Then— something went wrong with the car. (*MANUAL SOUND TWO: Gears jamming. Starter button dead. SOUND RECORDING: Train chugging up, louder.*) The train was coming closer. I could hear the cry of its whistle. (*SOUND RECORDING: Train chugging. Cry of whistle closer. All of this should be a cacophony of sound blended together, almost overriding the driver's voice, which tries to rise above it, almost hysterical with panic.*) Still he stood there. And now—I knew that he was beckoning—beckoning me to my death . . .

HITCH-HIKER: (*Hollowly off-stage through megaphone*) Hall . . . ooo
. . . Hall . . . oo . . . (*SOUND RECORDING: Auto starting. Auto hum
steady up. Music continuing.*)

ADAMS: . . . . He began to be everywhere. Wherever I stopped, even
for a moment—for gas, for oil, for a drink of pop, a cup of coffee, a
sandwich—he was there. (*Music continuing. Auto sound continuing.
More tense and rapid.*) I saw him standing outside the auto camp in
Amarillo, that night, when I dared to slow down. He was sitting near
the drinking fountain in a little camping spot just inside the border
of New Mexico. . . . (*Music steady. Rapid, more breathless.*) He was
waiting for me outside the Navajo Reservation where I stopped to
check my tires. I saw him in Albuquerque, where I bought twenty
gallons of gas. I was afraid now, afraid to stop. I began to drive faster
and faster. I was in lunar landscape now—the great arid mesa country of New Mexico. I drove through it with the indifference of a fly
crawling over the face of the moon. . . . (*Auto hum up. Music more
and more eerie. More desperately.*) But now he didn't even wait for
me to stop. Unless I drove at eighty-five miles an hour over those
endless roads, he waited for me at every other mile. I would see
his figure, shadowless, flitting before me, still in its same attitude,
over the cold lifeless ground, flitting over dried-up rivers, over broken stones cast up by old glacial upheavals, flitting in the pure and
cloudless air. . . . (*Music reaches eerie climax. Stops. Sound recording of auto hum stops. A low voice in the silence.*) I was beside myself
when I finally reached Gallup, New Mexico, this morning . . .

THE AIR-CONDITIONED
NIGHTMARE

HENRY MILLER

– 1945 –

----

*Just as Washington Irving had, over a century before him, Henry Miller
set out to rediscover America. The East Coast was confining him, "like a
rat trap: my one thought is to get out of New York, to experience something genuinely American." He did so by taking Route 66 west.*

*In 1939, after ten years as an expatriate, Miller returned to America and
took that "California trip." In the next excerpt, his dubious plan is to drive
66 across western Arizona, pass the Grand Canyon, and then cross the Mojave in one go. He drives the most rugged stretch of Route 66, the two-lane
road up and over Sitgreaves Pass, which he heard was "the worst spot on
Highway 66. Not too many miles to get to the top, if you get over it ok."*

*Miller's desire to know America, and his turning to Route 66 to find it,
reminds us that by 1949 this road had already entered popular and literary culture. F. Scott Fitzgerald wrote, "There are no second acts in American lives," yet that was the credo of those arriving in the West. Miller,
like Steinbeck after him in* Travels with Charley, *found only what he'd
brought with him: an easterner's trepidation regarding the West.*

The best-known novels of Henry Miller, Tropic of Cancer *(1934) and*
Tropic of Capricorn *(1939), were banned as obscene until 1961 in the
U.S. and U.K. This led him to the exile, which he broke with* The Air-
Conditioned Nightmare *(1945) and his trip along Route 66. His autobio-
graphical novels had a bohemian, liberating effect on American culture
in the 1960s.*

Once I got out of the forest and into the no-man's land where the mountains are wine-colored, the earth pea green, the mesas pink, blue, black and white, everything was lovely. For about forty miles I don't think I passed a human habitation. But that can happen of course most anywhere west of the big cities.

Only here it's terrifying. Three cars passed me and then there was a stretch of silence and emptiness, a steady, sinister ebbing of all human life, of plant and vegetable life, of light itself. Suddenly, out of nowhere, it seemed, three horsemen galloped into the center of the road about fifty yards ahead of me. They just materialized, as it were. For a moment I thought it might be a hold-up. But no, they pranced a moment or two in the middle of the road, waved me a greeting, and then spurred their horses on into the phantasmal emptiness of dusk, disappearing in the space of a few seconds. What was amazing to me was that they seemed to have a sense of direction; they galloped off as if they were going somewhere when obviously there was nowhere to go. When I got to Cameron I nearly passed it. Luckily there was a gas station, a few shacks, a hotel and some hogans by the side of the road. "Where's Cameron?" I asked, thinking it lay hidden on the other side of the bridge. "You're in it," said the man at the gas station. I was so fascinated by the eeriness of the décor that before inquiring for a room I walked down to the Little Colorado River and took a good look at the canyon there. I didn't know until the next morning that I was camping beside the Painted Desert . . .

Ever since I hit Tucumcari I have become completely disoriented. On the license plates in New Mexico it reads: "The Land of Enchantment." And that it is, by God! There's a huge rectangle which embraces parts of four States—Utah, Colorado, New Mexico and Arizona—and which is nothing but enchantment, sorcery, illusionismus, phantasmagoria. Perhaps the secret of the American continent is contained in this wild, forbidding and partially unexplored territory. It is the land of the Indian par excellence. Everything is hypnagogic, chthonian and super-celestial. Here Nature has gone gaga and dada. Man is just an irruption, like a wart or a pimple. Man is not wanted here. Red men, yes, but then they are so far removed from what we think of as man that they seem like another species. Embedded in the rocks are their glyphs and hieroglyphs. Not to speak of the footprints of dinosaurs and other lumbering antediluvian beasts.

When you come to the Grand Canyon it's as though Nature were breaking out into supplication. On an average it's only ten to eighteen miles from rim to rim of the Canyon, but it takes two days to traverse it on foot or horseback. It takes four days for the mail to travel from one side to the other, a fantastic journey in which your letters pass through four States. Animals and birds rarely cross the abyss. The trees and vegetation differ from one plateau to the other. Passing from top to bottom you go through practically all the climatic changes known on the globe, except the Arctic and Antarctic extremes. Between two formations of rock there was, so the scientists say, an interval of 500,000,000 years.

It's mad, completely mad, and at the same time so grandiose, so sublime, so illusory, that when you come upon it for the first time you break down and weep with joy. I did, at least. For over thirty years I had been aching to see this huge hole in the earth . . .

I was just entering the desert that lies between Needles and Barstow. It was six o'clock in the cool of a desert morning and I was sitting on the running board waiting for the engine to cool off. This repeated itself at regular intervals, every twenty or thirty miles, as I said before. When I had covered about fifty miles or so the car slowed down of itself, found its natural rhythm, as it were, and nothing I could do would make it change its pace. I was condemned to crawl along at twenty to twenty-five miles an hour.

When I got to a place called Amboy, I believe it was, I had a cool, consoling chat with an old desert rat who was the incarnation of peace, serenity and charity. "Don't fret yourself," he said. "You'll get there in good time. If not to-day why to-morrow. It makes no difference." Someone had stolen his peanut slot machine during the night. It didn't disturb him in the least. He put it down to human nature. "Some folks make you feel like a king," he said, "and others are lower than worms. We learn a lot about human nature watching the cars pass by." He had warned me that there would come a forty-mile stretch which would seem like the longest forty miles I had ever covered. "I've done it hundreds of times," he said, "and each time the miles seem to stretch out more and more."

HISPANIC ON ROUTE 66

RUDOLFO ANAYA

— 1950s —

Hispanic Americans, who descended from migrations northward, Native settlers, and Spanish explorers, lived and worked the land, and intermarried. Route 66 was once a land of ranchos and haciendas.

After the Okie and Arkie migration thinned, a new breed crossed the thirty-fifth parallel. People seeking adventure rather than sanctuary: tourists. They traveled not for a job or a place to live. No, they were on 66 "para conocer"—to know the great expanse of the American land. Memories of Route 66 have focused on accounts of the traveler and the tourist, but what of those left behind in the swirling dust? Those whose experience with cars was limited to the ones stopping at the local gas station or those who never knew the feel of fresh sheets in a tourist court or hotel?

Rudolfo Anaya has been described in the New York Times *as "the most widely read Hispanic author in America today." The author of dozens of volumes, his work ranges from essays to drama to travel lore. He is best known as the author of the novel* Bless Me, Ultima *(1972), in which he writes passionately about the struggle of a child to trying to know himself, his family, his place. In the encounter told here, Anaya gives a background to Hispanic identity on Route 66.*

M y parents were both born in a small village in the Pecos River valley, a village by the name of Puerto de Luna. My father was a cowboy, I guess you'd say. He worked with cattle. And my mother's family was from the river valley. They were farmers.

We moved [along Route 66] to Albuquerque in 1952, mostly in search of the future. Small towns in New Mexico have little to offer kids who are graduating from high school. There are no jobs, and so we followed very much the migration pattern of many families in the '50s into the big cities. Albuquerque was opening up then, a postwar city . . .

I don't have to return to Europe or to Spain specifically for roots or for cultural identity. I have it right here in the New World. And I think once I define that for myself and know it within myself, it gives me a great deal of satisfaction in one way and a great deal of authenticity in another. I've come to a point where I can really say to myself, "I know who I am, and I don't have to go out searching for bloodlines that don't exist, or if they do exist, mean very little. I am very much a New Mexican, and take my perspective from this little corner of the New World.

There is a tension involved in Hispanic writing and in Hispanic culture—it is a tension because it is a way of identity, of trying to identify. What we have to do in our Hispanic community in the Southwest is to read our history, to know our history . . .

There's a new Hispanic culture emerging in the cities. One of the most powerful symbols that unites the Spanish world with the Meso-American world is La Virgen de Guadalupe, and you put it on a lowrider, customized beautiful car that's going up and down Central [Route 66]. If we can keep enough of that attachment, and knowledge of the symbols and of the history, then we're all right, we'll survive . . .

I think one of the things that writers have not dared to do enough in the Southwest is to study racism and prejudices in our area. What we preach is more of, "We're getting along wonderfully, aren't we?" We have distinct cultures that lend to each other and work with each other, and I think that's a positive message, but it's not completely true. . . . You cannot be Chicano or Hispanic in this country, unfortunately I know this, and not have felt racism.

I remember my early years in grade school, and I have a story about Route 66.

I grew up off Route 66, on the eastern llano of New Mexico. The first tourists I ever encountered were on 66, right after World War II. People were moving west. One afternoon at a gas station where we went to fill our bike tires after goathead punctures, a car stopped. Dad, mom, son, and daughter: blue-eyed gringos from the East. They usually didn't pay attention to the brown Mexicanitos gathered at the gas station, but this Ozzie and Harriet Nelson couple did . . .

"Where are you from?" Ozzie asked.

"Here," I said.

"Just here?" he said looking around.

"Yes." I had never considered any place other than just here. Here was home.

"Oh," he said, and went off to kick his car's tires.

"Where are you from?" I asked Harriet.

"Back east."

"Where are you going?" I asked.

"We're tourists," she answered. "We're going to California."

Imagine, I thought to myself. A family can travel to California as tourists. Just to go look! I knew then that I wanted to be a tourist.

I ran home and told my mother, "Mama, I want to be a tourist."

Her mouth dropped. She stopped rolling tortillas and made the sign of the cross over me. "Where did you get that idea?"

I told her about the family I had just met.

"No, *mijito*," she said. "Only the Americanos can be tourists. Now go help Ultima with her herbs."

EAST BOUND

(5)

DESERT AND COASTAL 66

CALIFORNIA

R. WALDMIRE 4.91

El Garces, Needles, California

GUNSLINGER

ED GORMAN

— 1920s —

Ranch hands and dime-store cowboys traveled Route 66, back in the days of matinees at the picture theater: Hopalong Cassidy, Gabby Hayes, and Gene Autry, the Singing Cowboy. The 66 mystique seems irresistible to filmmakers. Route 66 is featured or pictured in three or four dozen popular American films, everything from science fiction (Attack of the 50 Foot Woman, 1958), *to horror* (Kalifornia, 1993).

This excerpt is a western, a genre that whole generations associate with buttery popcorn and sticky floors. Route 66 had more than its share of six-guns and pounding hooves in a canyon. Victorville, California, and Gallup, New Mexico, were both sites of dozens of "oaters." The horse operas were shot with real dust blowing and genuine sagebrush, but the gear arrived via Route 66. In this story, Gorman evokes the magic of Hollywood's silent-film days in the twenties. There's a cowboy at the door of Hollywood 66, *planning to assassinate director Thomas Ince, who may be an extra on his own set.*

Ed Gorman, a crime noir, mystery, suspense, and western writer, has written more that twenty novels, five collections of short stories, and three screenplays, including What Dead Men Say (1990), The Day the Music Died (1999), *and* A Ticket to Ride (2009). *He is also a founding editor of the mystery genre magazine* Mystery Scene.

H e finds a rooming house two blocks from a bar called The Water-hole, which is where most of the cowboys hang out. Because real ranches in the west have fallen on hard times, the cowboys had little choice but to drift to Los Angeles to become extras and stunt riders and trick shooters in the silent movie industry. Now there is a whole colony, a whole sub-culture of them out here, and they are much given to drink and even more given to violence. So he must be careful around them, very careful . . .

In the Los Angeles of the movie cowboy extra, there are certain key places to go for work. On Sunset Boulevard there is a horse barn where you wait like farmhands to be picked for a day's work; then there are a few studio backlots where you can stand in the baking sun all day waiting for somebody already hired to keel over and need to be replaced; and then there is Universal's slave-galley arrangement where extras are literally herded into a big cage to wait to be called. Five dollars a day is the pay, which for some men is five times what they were getting back in the blizzard country of Montana and Wyoming and Utah.

It is into this world he slips now, making the rounds, trying to get himself hired as an extra. If he does not get on Ince's set Thursday, if he does not get that close, then he will be unable to do what he has waited most of his life to do.

He is accepted. Or at least none of the other cowboys question him. They talk in their rough boozy way of doing stunt work—something called the "Running W" or the even more frightening "Dead Man's Fall" are particularly popular topics—and they gossip about the movie stars themselves. Which sweet young virginal types can actually be had by just about anybody who has taken a bath in the past month. Which so-called he-men are actually prancing nancies afraid to even get close to a horse.

All this fascinates and frightens him. He wants to be back home in Morgan County, Missouri.

All that keeps him going is the memory of his father. The pennies on Father's eyes during the wake. The waxen look in the coffin. The smell of funeral flowers. His mother weeping, weeping.

The Navy Colt burs in his waistband. Burns . . .

Late on Wednesday, near the corral on the Miller Brothers 101 Ranch where Ince makes his two-reelers, a fat bald casting director in jodhpurs comes over and says, "You five men there. Can you be here at sunup?"

He has traveled fifteen hundred miles and forty-one years for this moment.

THE HIGH WINDOW

RAYMOND CHANDLER

— 1942 —

The next two selections are detective stories in the noir tradition, one each from before and after World War II. Chandler's The High Window *is a tale of gold fever. Not the gold for which Beale and his camels surveyed a wagon road, but a more portable form: a rare solid-gold doubloon. The woman who owns the coin hires Philip Marlowe, the legendary private eye of fiction, to find it. He does, but then she claims to have the coin herself! Gold has always lurked in tales of the Golden State and its California Dream, whether told by explorers or by the smart-aleck detectives of this story.*

The locations in this story—Sunset Boulevard, the Pasadena Freeway—are both part of Route 66 in Los Angeles. How Marlowe travels the maze seems less of a challenge than his negotiating the demands of clients. When a client complained that she didn't like his attitude, he replied, "I don't like it either." He's a character, and as one observer in the following excerpt notes, "Hollywood's full of them." And so is Route 66.

The Philip Marlowe mysteries of Raymond Chandler are few but well known: The Big Sleep *(1939),* Farewell, My Lovely *(1940),* The High Window *(1942),* The Lady in the Lake *(1943),* The Little Sister *(1949),* The Long Goodbye *(1953), and* Playback *(1958). Chandler also wrote such classic films as* Double Indemnity *(1944),* The Blue Dahlia *(1946), and* Strangers on a Train *(1951).*

I drove west on Sunset, fiddled around a few blocks without making up my mind whether anyone was trying to follow me, then parked near a drugstore and went into its phone booth. I dropped my nickel and asked the O-operator for a Pasadena number. She told me how much money to put in.

The voice which answered the phone was angular and cold. "Mrs. Murdock's residence."

"Philip Marlowe here. Mrs. Murdock, please."

I was told to wait. A soft but very clear voice said: "Mr. Marlowe? Mrs. Murdock is resting now. Can you tell me what it is?"

"You oughtn't to have told him."

"I—who—?"

"That loopy guy whose handkerchief you cry into."

"How dare you?"

"That's fine," I said. "Now let me talk to Mrs. Murdock. I have to."

"Very well. I'll try." The soft clear voice went away and I waited a long wait. They would have to lift her up on the pillows and drag the port bottle out of her hard gray paw and feed her the telephone. A throat was cleared suddenly over the wire. It sounded like a freight train going through a tunnel.

"This is Mrs. Murdock."

"Could you identify the property we were talking about this morning, Mrs. Murdock? I mean could you pick it out from others just like it?"

"Well—are there others just like it?"

"There must be. Dozens, hundreds for all I know. Anyhow dozens. Of course I don't know where they are."

She coughed. "I don't really know much about it. I suppose I couldn't identify it then. But in the circumstances—"

"That's what I'm getting at, Mrs. Murdock. The identification would seem to depend on tracing the history of the article back to you. At least to be convincing."

"Yes. I suppose it would. Why? Do you know where it is?"

"Morningstar claims to have seen it. He says it was offered to him for sale—just as you suspected. He wouldn't buy. The seller was not a woman, he says. That doesn't mean a thing, because he gave me a detailed description of the party which was either made up or was a description of somebody he knew more than casually. So the seller may have been a woman."

I would probably have gone on like that for a long time, not knowing just what I was trying to say, if she hadn't stopped me with a noise like a seal barking. "This is all very unnecessary now, Mr. Marlowe. I have decided to drop the matter. The coin has been returned to me."

"Hold the wire a minute," I said. I put the phone back on the shelf and opened the booth door and stuck my head out, filling my chest with what they were using for air in the drugstore. Nobody was paying any attention to me. Up front the druggist, in a pale blue smock, was chatting across the cigar counter. The counter boy was polishing glasses at the fountain. Two girls in slacks were playing the pinball machine. A tall narrow party in a black shirt and a pale yellow scarf was fumbling magazines at the rack. He didn't look like a gunman.

I pulled the booth shut and picked up the phone and said: "A rat was gnawing my foot. It's all right now. You got it back, you said. Just like that. How?"

"I hope you are not too disappointed," she said in her uncompromising baritone. "The circumstances are a little difficult. I may decide to explain and I may not. You may call at the house tomorrow morning. Since I do not wish to proceed with the investigation, you will keep the retainer as payment in full."

"Let me get this straight," I said. "You actually got the coin back—not a promise of it, merely?"

"Certainly not. And I'm getting tired. So, if you—"

"One moment, Mrs. Murdock. It isn't going to be as simple as all that. Things have happened."

"In the morning you may tell me about them," she said sharply, and hung up.

I pushed out of the booth and lit a cigarette with thick awkward fingers. I went back along the store. The druggist was alone now. He was sharpening a pencil with a small knife, very intent, frowning.

"That's a nice sharp pencil you have there," I told him.

He looked up, surprised. The girls at the pinball machine looked at me, surprised. I went over and looked at myself in the mirror behind the counter. I looked surprised. I sat down on one of the stools and said: "A double Scotch, straight."

The counter man looked surprised. "Sorry, this isn't a bar, sir. You can buy a bottle at the liquor counter."

"So it is," I said. "I mean, so it isn't. I've had a shock. I'm a little dazed. Give me a cup of coffee, weak, and a very thin ham sandwich on stale bread. No, I better not eat yet either. Good-by."

I got down off the stool and walked to the door in a silence that was as loud as a ton of coal going down a chute. The man in the black shirt and yellow scarf was sneering at me over the *New Republic*. "You ought to lay off that fluff and get your teeth into something solid, like a pulp magazine," I told him, just to be friendly.

I went out. Behind me somebody said: "Hollywood's full of them."

INDIAN FARM-WORKERS ON 66

LOUIS OWENS

– 1960s –

Route 66 served not only to bring tourists and travelers to Indian reserva-
tions, but also as a road where an Indian could drive without licenses
or police patrols. For Louis Owens, born to a family of Indian migrant
workers, 66 was a road to savor, a break before hitting California's famous
factories in the fields.

Louis Owens grew up to become a Steinbeck scholar, a well-received
novelist, and a full professor at the largest university on Route 66, the
University of New Mexico. His journey is a dramatic one, written in
Route 66's ruts, and he sees the Route 66 saga in broad historical terms:
both its gritty reality and its TV shellacking. Few scholars of Route 66 (or
of John Steinbeck, or of California literature) grew up picking vegetables
as Owens did. The experience sharpened his insights into the hype and
legendry of 66.

Louis Owens published fiction with autobiographical themes, and an
essay on Route 66. The list includes The Sharpest Sight *(1993),* Bone
Game *(1994),* Wolfsong *(1995),* Nightland *(1997), which won the Ameri-*
can Book Award, and Dark River *(1999). This interview was conducted by*
this volume's editor, a colleague, before Owens's untimely death in 2002.

My father's Choctaw and Cajun French and Irish. My mother's
family are Cherokee and Irish from Oklahoma. My father left
Mississippi when he was fifteen and joined the army. Ended up sta-

tioned in Lompoc, California, where I was born. For the next seven years we yo-yoed back and forth between the Yazoo River and Mississippi and California because after my father got out of the military, he became a farm-worker in California. When we lived in California, we actually lived in a tent encampment in Delano, in the Central Valley, much like the Joads, probably. We gleaned potatoes. We hoed—beans, sugar peas—picked tomatoes.

Steinbeck pursued this issue of the troubles in California ensuing from the migration of the so-called "Okies." There was a story that Steinbeck actually drove Route 66—the route of the Joads. That may be apocryphal. If you read *The Grapes of Wrath*, what you see is a man who sat down with a map and looked at all the colorful names along Route 66 on the map—and wrote them into a litany in the novel.

I think he made it the spine of the novel because it was the dominant route that most of the migrants took out of the so-called Dust Bowl—into California. That's where they drove—that's the route that my family and I drove many times between California and Mississippi. It was pretty much a poor person's route. So, it simply made sense: if he was going to write about the phenomenon of the Dust Bowl and the Okies, that's how he structured it; and, of course, it's the perfect structure for that kind of novel—it's a journey novel.

Steinbeck writes brilliantly about America—the American metanarrative—the American myth. This is really a migration story—the movement from east to west.

From Steinbeck on, the road becomes a road that epitomizes that aspect of the American dream associated with freedom or escape. The old dream of better life, better possibilities—you know, the dream that resulted in Walt Whitman in his great poem "Facing West from California's Shores"—Standing there looking west across the Pacific and saying, "But where is what I started for, so long ago? And why is it yet unfound?" You know, it's that dream.

So, in that sense, it hasn't changed at all: when you watched that TV series *Route 66* and saw the two guys in the Corvette picking dates and their various itinerant labors along the roads. It's the dream of freedom, but it's a dream of a possible new life, always before you.

According to Steinbeck, it's a dream that panders to all of us. It's a false dream. It's not just an illusion or delusion—but it's dangerous because what you do is you keep moving west and keep leaving the old world behind and used up and worn out and poisoned and destroyed because there's always more to the West.

During the Dust Bowl, when my mother's family came out from Oklahoma, they came out to California along with other migrants. A lot of those people were Indian. There is a Native history, a Native American history to the Route 66 migration. Steinbeck touches on this in *The Grapes of Wrath* when Tom Joad meets the Cherokee man in the government camp at Weedpatch. Steinbeck makes a mistake there; he didn't get his fact straight about Indians and reservations.

Yes, Route 66 has been "whitened." The conclusion I've come to is to see that we're selling a product here. Whether it's a television show—such as *Route 66*—or a novel, or a film, we're selling that product to consumers. The consumers, people with the money, the leisure time, etcetera—are not African American, Native American, Hispanic American, Asian American—at least not in consciousness of large producers. They're selling to a market that's predominantly Anglo-European. It makes sense to put a show on television with white guys in a Corvette because of who's watching those shows.

The problem is if you aren't one of those two Anglo-Saxon guys jetting around in your Corvette and you happen to have dark skin; if, for example, your parents happen to have been field workers, or maybe English isn't your first language, you don't see yourself there. You don't see yourself reflected back from any of the media, whether it's a television screen, a movie, or a book. So, you don't find the place for yourself in this country.

I think you're doing it with your anthology and memoir [*Across the Tracks: A Route 66 Story*]. This is extremely important. Maybe with the changing consciousness people will start to look around and see things they didn't see before. We're dealing with a situation that Ralph Ellison wrote about in *Invisible Man*, in which a black man is invisible unless he assumes the role the white world expects to see. The white man becomes that drop of black that makes the white whiter—the paint in Ralph Ellison's novel. The dominant culture doesn't see people who don't look like them unless representations change. I think we have got to have books, films, TV shows that show the real world—show the black farmer in Oklahoma along Route 66 and so on. How to package and market that to the American public is still a big question.

My earliest memories—almost pre-memories—are traveling that

road. We'd be in some kind of rattletrap car that had canvas water bag hanging from every projection. Water bags off the radiator cap and water bags off the mirrors and door handles, and any place that was jagged enough to hold a canvas water bag because you didn't want to break down without water.

Long, long trips. I remember you could stop in Oklahoma or Texas for free watermelon. There were watermelon stands set up, and they would give you slices of watermelon. We camped beside the road and cooked fried potatoes. I never stayed in a motel until I was an adult. My family would have never thought about it. It was always a frightening adventure—a dreamlike experience as well because we were always in constant motion, which could be interrupted at any second by a blown valve, or a radiator that went out, or two flat tires or whatever.

I can remember flocks of sheep crossing Route 66 and stopping us. We had to stop and watch Navajo sheepherders while their dogs took their sheep across for twenty minutes or however long it took. I can remember flash floods that cut Route 66, stranded us for a day or two. It was always motion, and it was always along that road passing through Albuquerque—passing through Amarillo, and so on. It's a wonderful memory.

I can remember being a child and arriving at the bridges spanning the Mississippi, and my father didn't have enough money—I think it was twenty-five or cents to pay the fare to get across the bridge. We had driven from California to Mississippi, arrived at the Mississippi, without twenty-five or thirty-five cents to get across. That's the kind of road Route 66 is, I think, for people at the bottom of economic scale in America. It's an essential road, a life road, but it's a risky road. It's not a pleasure cruise. It's not a hipster's jaunt, as Kerouac saw it, or a cruise in a Corvette or the road of the myth, as Europeans probably see it. It's a necessary and difficult path.

THE MUSIC OF 66

RY COODER

— 1950s —

Route 66 is cemented into popular culture. Whether you're from a generation who remembers the Joads and their jalopy, or a TV series with two crew cuts in Corvettes, or the Pixar movie Cars, *three generations have fixed this road in their mind as something special and something American.*

Songs have always been a big part of 66's appeal, from the Dust Bowl ballads of Woody Guthrie and others, to the tune "Get Your Kicks on Route 66," as popularized by Nat King Cole in the 1940s and now recorded in more than one hundred versions from punk to salsa.

Ry Cooder has been driving and singing about Route 66 and its travelers since childhood. His love for the road is a personal experience. 66 has a ghostlike reality to him, which he enlivens, verse after verse, in such albums as Into the Purple Valley, Boomer's Story, *and* Paradise and Lunch. *A consummate instrumentalist, he has popularized old songs to new audiences, just as he brought Cuban music to North America with his film and album* Buena Vista Social Club.

In the '30s, railroading began to fall off in its scope and number of miles, and the amount of equipment used. They didn't have much of a highway system in this country then. Route 66 was mud and dirt, and it was hard to get from out there to out here, so the trains were the main thing, and "boomers" were the guys, the train workers who were put off [the job]. They were union men, and apparently the unions were broken up by the train companies. Organized labor was under attack because it had gotten big and powerful. And so these train men would be put off the trains, but what they did do, they continued to ride the trains as hobos, and they were called "boomers." As the song "Boomer's Story" says, "I hear another train a-comin' / Guess I'll be on my way." That's about the size of it; they never stayed very long in one place.

During the Depression, hobos became greater in number and more of a problem. They were considered bums and no-account and bad people. But the boomers had a certain honor and a certain status. These were simply guys who had a job, had a calling and a profession, and then they didn't have it anymore. It was not their fault.

Who writes songs like "Boomer's Story?" It's obviously not written by a professional songwriter. It's not a Tin Pan Alley song, yet it's far from being a rustic song, too. It's not a hymn-tune structure like many of the nineteenth-century cowboy tunes. Not popular music converted into cowboy music. It's an early example of modern American narrative songwriting, which I just love a lot.

So, when I was making those early records, I had been so crazy about those tunes all my life that I thought, "Well, this is what I'll do, I'll just sing these things and make little interesting arrangements out of them." Of course very few people cared. This was the '70s and this was not what was going on in pop music or what record companies were interested in, by any means.

Then there's that tune, "How Can You Keep On Moving?" That's a fabulous song—an authentic Okie ballad—written by Sis [Agnes] Cunningham. There again, not a rustic song and not a professional song but very telling: concise, coherent, and funny—very ironic and funny. It asks the question, "How can you keep on moving unless you migrate, too?" They told them, "Keep moving; don't migrate!" That's what they said to all the pickers and Okies and Arkies and everybody who came out looking for work. It was *The Grapes of Wrath*: "Don't stop here! Don't let the sun set on you! There is no place to stay." And they wanted them to work, of course, for less and less money.

I don't know any tune like that as good, except, of course, Woody Guthrie. Take "Do Re Mi":

> *Lots of folk back east, they say*
> *Are leaving home ev'ryday,*
> *Beatin' the hot old dusty way*
> *To the California line.*

And how they did that was to go on 66, and then they'd get told the same idea as "How Can You Keep On Moving?" Guthrie's telling the people back home that you had better stay put, if you can.

> *You'd better stay right where you are.*
> *You'd better take this little tip from me,*
> *'Cause I look through the want ads every day*
> *And the headlines in the paper always say . . .*

They found themselves in a terrible jam, these guys, so many of them, who have now settled in California and live in the San Joaquin Valley (or their descendants do). Or up north in Humboldt County. Sometimes their descendants became successful, sometimes not.

This Dust Bowl thing started up, and everybody went west on 66. You know, that country down there was emptied out. All these farmers just had to go. What a strange experience, you know. I love the song "The Great Dust Storm":

> *On the fourteenth day of April, 1935,*
> *You could see the dust storms coming,*
> *A mighty cave of black . . .*

It just must have been unbelievable. And "So Long, It's Been Good to Know Yuh":

> *The dust blotted out the sun.*
> *Straight for home all the people did run.*
> *Singin': So long, it's been good to know yuh.*

The preacher's leaving. The sweethearts are saying goodbye. Everybody's heading out. Guthrie really was able to tell that story in the vernacular of the people.

If you asked me to name a dozen or so of the great American songs,

I'm going to include Bobby Troup's "Get Your Kicks on Route 66," because it does everything a song should do. It rocks like mad. It's fast moving. It's got action in it. It's very hard to write a song in which the lyrics and the tempo and the melody move you—that actually gives you a sense of going. The first and greatest thing about this song is that you feel like you're in the car—I'm thinking about a lime-green '53 Cadillac with a big motor and leather seats. And then he hits all the places, you know, along the way. And he makes it rhyme. And he makes the towns sound so good. You oughta see Amarillo—God, what an awful place. Oklahoma, New Mexico—those places are rough. "Don't forget Winona." Most people never heard of Winona, let alone forget it. It's very funny.

When I was, let's see, five, six, seven, eight years old, I heard these records, the Folkways records. Moe Asch had the genius to package these records along with WPA photographs by Dorothea Lange. The photographs of the people and their journey, together with the songs—for a white kid from Santa Monica—this very exotic music and these pictures were so remarkable to me. I thought, "My God, this is fantastic. Who is this singing and what is this all about? Did this really happen? When was this?"

It seemed so strange and beautiful, and my father had come out with his family in the '20s from back east, and they drove. He used to talk about that.

When you are little and you are impressed by something, you build up images of it and yourself and how you coincide with it. If you went to get off the sidewalks of Santa Monica and the stupid intersections and the dumbbell school I had to go to, music was a good way to go.

You can't physically travel at age five. I'm not going to go hobo down Route 66, much as I would have liked to. Then, when I got older, my dad would take me out to the desert. To just be out in the desert—now it's full of K-marts and malls and things, our poor Mojave is being overrun—but in those days it was still pretty nice, pristine.

There was no Route 66 organization, and there was no club and there was no thought about it. And pretty soon there were Interstates 40 and 15, and they bypassed 66. But we used to go out there and drive around—you're speaking of a journey that happened in my head, you know? Then I began to collect pictures of my own and magazines.

Nowadays you can go buy wonderful books on the Mother Road;

there's quite a bibliography. (I've got a lot of books about Route 66.) But in those days, in the '50s, it was not thought about. There was nothing retro yet, see? But the records did it and thank God for those Folkways records. They were it in those days. There wasn't anything else.

I had a banjo, and it was too loud, and it gave me a headache, so I sold it, and took the money—and I was about seventeen—and I bought this Packard, this '47 Packard. It was fantastic—big, enormous, straight-eight, four-door sedan. It was like a train, you know, a club car on a train with velour seats and—oh, it was wonderful. Big white-walled tires. So I used to go out in that car and just go, just drive. And pretend.

SOUL IN THE DESERT

ROBERT ERVIN

— 1950s —

Officially closed in 1985, Route 66 still has as many surprises, dead ends, and contradictions as it has potholes. For every stereotypical roadside attraction snaring tourists, there is the real thing—a café built out of rocks or a plaster gorilla smiling down on motorists. "Do I contradict myself?" Walt Whitman asked. "Yes, I contain multitudes." This is a story about these multitudes, which Carl Sandburg wrote of in The People, Yes.

"Occasionally a black traveler stops at my general store," exclaims Robert Ervin, who gave up the city for a remote California town on an old alignment of Route 66 in the Mojave. "They stare and they say, 'What's a brother doing here!'" Whether they stopped for a burger or to marvel at the catfish pond he dug in back, Ervin is another of the surprises along the way. Here, he reminds us of the struggles African American travelers found on 66, which prompted publication of Green's guide.

Robert Ervin grew up in the American South, before his family moved to Los Angeles where he graduated from college and received his master's degree in counseling from UCLA. His general store on the original alignment of Route 66, in a desert whistle-stop named Goffs, in rural California, is currently closed.

I was born in Shreveport, Louisiana, back in 1936. My dad, he had a '40 Packard, old convertible, and we traveled Route 66 to California. We cooked up chicken before we left. You know, that's the first thing to do when black people get ready to travel, they go out and start wringing chicken necks. They were part of the travel gear. They told us we were moving to California, and they told us tales about California.

In the forties, California was mostly orange groves and everybody in California who wanted to work was working. My father, he had got out of the service here, and he had looked around, and the work was good. My father started driving out here, and, like I said, it wasn't as slow as the old wagon train, but it was slow because everyone drove a little careful, out here in this desert.

It was like an old fairy tale. They were taking off the old and looking forward to the new. And so we'd stop and talk to people about where were they going when they got to California. There was no I-40 over there; there was no I-10. Route 66 was the only route through here, and the old railroad tracks were there then.

My sisters and I were really happy to leave, because my grandparents were very strict. We was in church all the time. We were in church six days a week. If we were bad, we had to go to seven.

Once on the route we went in to buy some Coke, sandwiches. . . . We were standing at the butcher counter. And this little girl walked over and looked at me, and she looked up at her mom and asked her mom, "Mom, is that a nigger?" And she got very embarrassed, and she looked at me, and she grabbed the little girl and rushed out of the store.

Yet, there were quite a few black servicemen. We were in east Los Angeles, in the Roman Gardens, where we moved. The Gardens, right now, it's just about ninety-nine percent Hispanics.

I played tennis for Compton High School, and I played basketball. I was an "A" student. But two weeks before graduation, all of a sudden, they decided that all these blacks were out of the school district, and they put us out. The next morning, they had about five busloads of NAACP members out in front of Compton High School. They took me back in school. I didn't march with my class, I was very despondent about that. That actually happened.

Goffs basically was a water stop for trains. This is with an uphill climb from Needles, this is 2,600 feet up. They built [Route 66] here because of the water stop, as well as the way it travels along the railroad.

The old cars then had a lot of vapor lock problems, which they don't have now. Through automation and engineering, they got things like that cleared up. But then, you saw people out there pouring Coca-Colas on the gas line, to free up the vapor lock.

You know, a lot of things we take for granted because there's so much of it now, and big cities are growing up. Then you could go for three, four, five hundred miles and nothing's in between. So you had to kind of figure out and plan things a lot better.

People got stuck. The only good thing about it, then, people were a lot more neighborly. Now, with things happening, people are afraid to stop.

BLUE TIME

EARLENE FOWLER

– 1960s –

If Route 66 has been about hard traveling for many—for Blacks, Indians, Hispanics, the Japanese interned there—it has also been hard for women traveling on their own. Sometimes the need to flee from a bad home has driven women to the road, as it did their foremothers who crossed the plains in wagons. This next story captures the dicey experiences of some female Route 66 travelers and the trade-offs they made in their search for a better life down the road. It's also an object lesson for its characters in the dangers of straying from the interstate and a straight and normal way of life.

Agatha Award–winner Earlene Fowler is the author of more than a dozen mystery novels, including Broken Dishes *(2004),* Delectable Mountains *(2005), and* Tumbling Blocks *(2007). She was raised in La Puente, California, by a southern mother and a western father. Her Benni Harper detective series is set in central California.*

Fleeing on Christmas Eve carrying your life savings of nine hundred thirteen dollars, a Toyota in need of a new carburetor, all your clothes and a few books, was sometimes a person's only viable option. With the holidays, they'd have a two-day start. Anyone could disappear in forty-eight hours . . .

It was five o'clock when they came to the small black-and-white road sign that said, "Historic Route 66." On a whim, tired of the whine of the interstate and the constant dodging of the big rigs rattling their old car with every pass, Em turned onto the small highway. She'd loved maps as a child, and travel stories, always wishing she was the person hitchhiking across America or driving the backroads like John Steinbeck in a homemade camper with a dog named Charlie. Though she'd never seen the old Route 66 television series, she read books on "The Mother Road."

She knew there were three little towns on this stretch of 66—Ludlow, Amboy, and Essex. The Ludlow Café had long since been abandoned, its white stucco surprisingly bare of graffiti. Driving along the two-lane highway, Em could see Interstate 40 in the distance, the colorful cars and trucks like Matchbox toys. It seemed appropriate to be on this old road, this less traveled highway. Interstate 40 was the real road now. The road normal people took. People who knew where they were going.

Fifteen minutes later, Jessie woke up. "What's going on?" she asked, her blackened eye only half open. "Where are we?"

"Just a small detour," Em said. "I'm tired of the freeway. The truckers are crazy trying to speed home for Christmas."

Jessie readjusted her seatbelt and stared out at the long stretch of two-lane highway. "It looks like the moon out here."

Em nodded. In the falling dusk, the dry, mesquite-covered desert did look like another planet.

"I'm hungry," Jessie declared. "We'll never find a place to eat out here. How long is this road?"

"It'll be a while. There's some beef jerky in my purse."

"I don't want any jerky," Jessie said, her voice petulant. "I want a hamburger and French fries. This is boring. Let's go back to the big road."

"Can't now. We're committed . . ."

"There's a place," Jessie said as they came to the small town of Amboy. Small was the operative word. Roy's Café sat next to a row of neat white cabins. When they pulled in front of the café, an old man was turning the sign to closed. He gave them an apologetic shrug and turned his back.

"Well, shit," Jessie said.

"We'll find something else," Em replied patiently.

"Right, like, where?" . . .

"I'll drive fast," Em said. "Eat some jerky. It'll help until we find something." This idea of taking off on Route 66 had turned out to be a bad one and Em was angry at herself for not sticking to her original plan. Up ahead, a long distance away, a light glowed.

"It better be a restaurant," Jessie answered, picking a piece of jerky out of her teeth with a green fingernail. "You got any dental floss?"

"Somewhere," Em said. She concentrated on the lights, willing them to be a café. She was surprised when they came upon the square, brick and stucco building. The sign read ESTA'S CAFÉ.

"Thank goodness," Jessie said, unbuckling her seatbelt before Em could get the car turned off. They were the only ones in the parking lot, which gave Em a nervous feeling deep in her stomach. One of the things she'd learned early being bounced from foster home to foster home was safety in numbers. Especially after dark.

"I don't know about this," Em said. "It can't be much further to the interstate hookup. Maybe we should wait."

"I'm not waiting one more minute," Jessie said, slamming the car door. "My head's already starting to hurt."

The café was small and warm with brown vinyl booths and red formica tables. Near the old cash register sat a small artificial Christmas tree. The ornaments were dime store cacti and coyotes. Lettered on a star-shaped tree topper was "Forgiveness was born on Christmas Day . . ."

Em and Jessie were halfway through their hamburgers when the man walked in. The old woman got up from her stool behind the counter, picked up a menu and said, "Sit anywhere you like."

The man was tall and skinny with a red and black scorpion tattoo on his hand. His denim jacket was black with grime on the sleeves. He sat at the counter, glancing briefly over at Em and Jessie, his pale eyes lingering longer on Jessie . . .

Em watched him warily. One thing she'd picked up in all those foster homes was a sixth sense about trouble and meanness. This man was both, she'd stake her savings on it.

SLEEP IN THE MOJAVE DESERT

SYLVIA PLATH

– 1960 –

The desert is no lady, a western saying goes, but to Sylvia Plath, it's not human at all. It's a place of dry fire and ancient memories of rain, a place of straight roads and long-ago dreams from the men and women who traveled there.

Sleeping out in the desert was a necessity for many Old 66 travelers, in order to cross the three-hundred-mile expanse separating Needles, California, and Victorville, where U.S. 66 begins its descent into the Los Angeles Basin. In the old days, boards were laid down over the sand. Then, as now, crossing the desert was a danger and a charm.

Travel at one's peril, Plath seems to say, in these short, sharp lines where she captures the spirit of the Mojave for those who pass here—this place where only the animals belong, fit for toads and lizards and snakes rather than men.

Sylvia Plath was a poet and novelist known for extraordinary sensitivity in her literary art in The Bell Jar *(1963),* Ariel *(1966), and other works. Her posthumous* The Collected Poems *won the 1982 Pulitzer Prize in poetry. Sylvia Plath and her husband, poet Ted Hughes, crossed the Mojave in the summer of 1959 on a trip from Pasadena to the Grand Canyon and then to the East Coast. This poem, following Wordsworth's advice for "emotion recollected in tranquility" was composed in England a year later, in July 1960.*

Out here there are no hearthstones,
Hot grains, simply. It is dry, dry.
And the air dangerous. Noonday acts queerly
On the mind's eye, erecting a line
Of poplars in the middle distance, the only
Object beside the mad, straight road
One can remember men and houses by.
A cool wind should inhabit those leaves
And a dew collect on them, dearer than money,
In the blue hour before sunup.
Yet they recede, untouchable as tomorrow,
Or those glittery fictions of spilt water
That glide ahead of the very thirsty.

I think of the lizards airing their tongues
In the crevice of an extremely small shadow
And the toad guarding his heart's droplet.
The desert is white as a blind man's eye,
Comfortless as salt. Snake and bird
Doze behind the old masks of fury.
We swelter like firedogs in the wind.

The sun puts its cinder out. Where we lie
The heat-cracked crickets congregate
In their black armorplate and cry.
The day-moon lights up like a sorry mother,
And the crickets come creeping into our hair
To fiddle the short night away.

SOME DREAMERS OF
THE GOLDEN DREAM

JOAN DIDION

– 1961 –

----

*Joan Didion's Route 66 is no Mother Road, and nowadays the only people
using it to flee seem to be those avoiding the traffic jams on the interstates of Southern California. Across the San Gabriel Valley, Route 66
has become a frontage road with a long string of strip malls. Flamboyant
in neon, replete with grifters, Route 66 is one long scar across the land,
sometimes terra-formed for a Spanish stucco, with a stagy front every bit
as fake as a Hollywood backlot.*

*In this rhinestone façade, Route 66 glitters but is not gold. Traffic
races through it at the pace of its red lights, and travelers are blown along
like leaves from a fall that never ceases. Above it all, indifferent to the
broken fan belts and fender-benders, a hot wind blows, like one of the
gates of Hell from which no soul returns, "the last stop for all those who
come from somewhere else."*

*Joan Didion is a leading stylist who has put Southern California on
the literary map. Her early books like* Play It as It Lays *(1970) and* The
White Album *(1979) documented California's urban culture.*

This is a story about love and death in the golden land, and begins
with the country. The San Bernardino Valley lies only an hour east
of Los Angeles by the San Bernardino Freeway but is in certain ways an
alien place: not the coastal California of the subtropical twilights and

the soft westerlies off the Pacific but a harsher California, haunted by the Mojave just beyond the mountains, devastated by the hot dry Santa Ana wind that comes down through the passes at 100 miles an hour and whines through the eucalyptus windbreaks and works on the nerves. October is the bad month for the wind, the month when breathing is difficult and the hills blaze spontaneously. There has been no rain since April. Every voice seems a scream. It is the season of suicide and divorce and prickly dread, wherever the wind blows.

The Mormons settled this ominous country, and then they abandoned it, but by the time they left the first orange tree had been planted and for the next hundred years the San Bernardino Valley would draw a kind of people who imagined they might live among the talismanic fruit and prosper in the dry air, people who brought with them Midwestern ways of building and cooking and praying and who tried to graft those ways upon the land. The graft took in curious ways. This is the California where it is possible to live and die without ever eating an artichoke, without ever meeting a Catholic or a Jew. This is the California where it is easy to Dial-A-Devotion, but hard to buy a book. This is the country in which a belief in the literal interpretation of Genesis has slipped imperceptibly into a belief in the literal interpretation of *Double Indemnity*, the country of the teased hair and the Capris and the girls for whom all life's promise comes down to a waltz-length white wedding dress and the birth of a Kimberly or a Sherry or a Debbi and a Tijuana divorce and a return to hairdressers' school. "We were just crazy kids," they say without regret, and look to the future. The future always looks good in the golden land, because no one remembers the past. Here is where the hot wind blows and the old ways do not seem relevant, where the divorce rate is double the national average and where one person in every thirty-eight lives in a trailer. Here is the last stop for all those who come from somewhere else, for all those who drifted away from the cold and the past and the old ways.

Imagine Banyan Street first, because Banyan is where it happened. The way to Banyan is to drive west from San Bernardino out Foothill Boulevard, Route 66: past the Santa Fe switching yards, the Forty Winks Motel. Past the motel that is nineteen stucco tepees: "SLEEP IN A WIGWAM—GET MORE FOR YOUR WAMPUM." Past Fontana Drag City and the Fontana Church of the Nazarene and the Pit Stop

A Go-Go; past Kaiser Steel, through Cucumonga, out to the Kapu Kai Restaurant-Bar and Coffee Shop, at the corner of Route 66 and Carnelian Avenue. Up Carnelian Avenue from the Kapu Kai, which means "Forbidden Seas," the subdivision flags whip in the harsh wind. "HALF-ACRE RANCHES! SNACK BARS! TRAVERTINE ENTRIES! $95 DOWN." It is the trail of an intention gone haywire, the flotsam of the New California.

Wigwam Motel, Rialto, California

SLEEPING BEAUTY

ROSS MACDONALD

– 1973 –

No one has created a detective quite so existential, nor a Southern Californian so fraught, as Ross McDonald, the pen name for Dr. Kenneth Millar. In this excerpt, detective Lew Archer befriends a young woman as mired in her troubles as a bird in an oil slick. Oil spills were common along the California coast in the early 1970s. Few made the connection between the oil oozing blackly along the beaches at the end of Route 66, and the cars that brought California its settlers and new residents.

In the back alleys of Route 66's Sunset Boulevard, a shadowy world lurks. It was the genius of Millar to situate our postwar fears of evil along some of the toniest stretches of Route 66 in California. Evil was there, all right, whether in the greed of oil producers, who accidentally spilled oil across the coast the author loved so much, or in the hands of the women who drift like fishes into an abandoned net. This is the world of Lew Archer—that Orion to the stars and detective to the rich and undeserving.

This is Coastal 66, where the oil coating the gulls turns into a dark vision of roman noir. Still, clients turn up, bodies are discovered, and the ending stretches of many a Route 66 journey turn bittersweet.

The wide reading that earned Kenneth Millar a doctorate in comparative literature also helped prune his sentences to a Hemingway-esque finish. A number of his novels were made into popular films, such as Blue City (with a sound track by Ry Cooder), The Moving Target (filmed as Harper), and The Drowning Pool.

The tide was coming in more strongly now, and I was afraid that the oil would come in with it. It might be on the beaches by tomorrow. I decided to go for a farewell walk southward along the shore. That happened to be the direction the woman with the grebe had taken.

The sunset spilled on the water and flared across the sky. The sky changed through several colors and became a soft crumbled gray. It was like walking under the roof of an enormous cave where hidden fires burned low. I came to a kind of natural corner where the shoreline curved out and a cliff rose abruptly from the beach. A few late surfers were waiting on the water for a final big one . . .

A white object was lodged high among the boulders. When I got nearer, I could see that it was a woman and hear between the sounds of the surf that she was crying. She turned her face away from me, but not before I recognized her.

As I came near, she sat perfectly still, pretending to be an accidental object caught in a crevice.

"Is there something the matter?"

She stopped crying with a gulp, as though she had swallowed her tears, and turned her face away. "No. There's nothing the matter."

"Did the bird die?"

"Yes. It died." Her voice was high and tight. "Now are you satisfied?"

"It takes a lot to satisfy me. Don't you think you should find a safer place to sit?"

She didn't respond at first. Then her head turned slowly. Her wet eyes gleamed at me in the deep twilight.

"I like it here. I hope the tide comes and gets me."

"Because one grebe died? A lot of diving birds are going to die."

"Don't keep talking about death. Please." She struggled out of her crevice and got to her feet. "Who are you anyway? Did somebody send you here to find me?"

"I came of my own accord." . . .

There were other people on the beach, talking in low tones or waiting in silence. We stood with them for a little while in the semidarkness. The ocean and its shores were never entirely dark: the water gathered light like the mirror of a telescope. The woman was standing so close to me I could feel her breath on my neck. Still she seemed a long way off, at a telescopic distance from me and the others. She seemed to feel it, too. She took hold of my hand. Her hand was cold.

She was shivering. I kept an old raincoat in the trunk of my car, and I got it out and put it over her shoulders. She didn't look at me or thank me . . .

On the way to Santa Monica, I listened to the morning news and learned that Lennox Oil was bringing in a wild-well team from Houston and preparing a major attempt to stop the spill. I switched off the radio and enjoyed the silence, broken only by the sounds of my own and other cars.

Traffic was still fairly light, and the day was clear enough to see the mountains rising in the east like the boundaries of an undiscovered country. I lapsed for a while into my freeway daydream: I was mobile and unencumbered, young enough to go where I had never been and clever enough to do new things when I got there.

The fantasy snapped in my face when I got to Santa Monica. It was just another part of the megapolis which stretched from San Diego to Ventura, and I was a citizen of the endless city. . . . The traffic below the window seemed to have a slightly anxious sound, as if it couldn't wait to get where it was going.

Chicago, Illinois

THE FUTURE OF 66

A ROCKET SCIENTIST LOOKS AT ROUTE 66'S FUTURE

PETER FRIEDMAN

— 2000 —

The future of Route 66 begins deep in its past. Generations earlier, railroad builders imagined a vast nation joined by iron rails. A half-century later, in the '20s, car manufacturers and owners, oil companies and merchants all fantasized about a good, all-weather road to join the Midwest and the West. Today, people cross continents to drive this road. What does the not-too-distant future hold for 66?

The future of Route 66 is still aborning: will it remain nostalgic, a compulsive "Our Town" look back on an America that was supposedly kinder and certainly slower? Will someone figure out how to enclose enough of Route 66 to call it a theme park?

But a road can't run only backwards in time. The transportation corridor of Route 66 has been heavily used by travelers for one hundred and fifty years. Who's to say that future vehicles—whether rocket cars or rockets—won't follow this well-traveled rut across the continent?

Peter Friedman holds a doctorate in physics from UC Berkeley. His work has ranged from supernovas to quantum electrodynamics theory and beyond. Friedman has used rockets for various projects, including one that mapped the hot and cold gases of our galaxy that cover over a quarter of the sky. Friedman currently explores the universe from Caltech, where he is a project scientist for NASA's Jet Propulsion Laboratory and at the Orbital Sciences Corporation.

I'm a physicist and I do astrophysics and research—mostly instrument building to take data from spaceborne instruments about our galaxy and other galaxies. People often refer to me as a rocket scientist, though to be fair I don't work on making rockets—I just use them.

There are the historic Route 66 signs that you see around campus [at the California Institute of Technology], and California Boulevard was at one point Route 66. That is the street below me—I'm just a few feet away. I'm most aware of it when I hear the song "Route 66"; I think, hey, I live there.

The next form of transportation on Route 66? Already there are plane routes that run from Chicago to L.A. Historic Route 66 was all over the place. It didn't stay tied down to where the train route was. In the same way, planes aren't tied down to following the road, they take the most convenient path based on whatever obstacles they have to stay away from.

Rockets on 66? It's possible. I wonder if the next step—at least sooner than rockets—would be ultrafast trains, TGV-type trains. I don't know when and if those are going to come to the U.S., but that technology exists in other countries and could get here long before rockets.

Though we could go faster on rockets, you could also go faster in a SST [Super Sonic Transport] like the Concorde, but that never turned out to be financially feasible.

My guess is that rocket-propelled transport for people on one place on the Earth to another place not that far away is probably not going to be cost-effective when you take into account safety and other parts of the economic equation.

Some of the planes tested in the past have been rocket planes that have been rocket-powered. Those were really just made to go up into space and back.

I'm not someone who has spent time looking at the economics of rocket flight, but I would guess that's still a long ways off. From what I know about space travel, there's a lot of dangers inherent in it and a lot of risk. So, for transportation of people and goods, it's not necessarily the way to go.

It's certainly plausible that rocket travel along Route 66 could happen within a century, but I guess it's beyond my event horizon. It's far enough away that I don't think we're going to see it in the next twenty or thirty years.

Will the Chicago-to-Los Angeles route be called "The Route 66 Special"? People come up with all sorts of names for rockets. Sometimes they're just numbers, but people with senses of humor who work on it could get names as elegant as some of the old train routes and Route 66. Between the song and other historical aspects it's something worthy of naming a rocket route.

ROGUE IN SPACE

FREDRIC BROWN

– Twenty-third century –

Can a road decommissioned more than a quarter-century ago have a future? Are kicks still to be had on 66? Route 66 has long served America and the world as an invitation to dream anew. Will this change as its roadway and sites crumble?

There are many ways to start over on Route 66. In this fantasy of the twenty-third century, a new way has emerged: sending criminals to the "psycher" for rehabilitation, where their memories are selectively wiped. This is not a bad analogy for one possible future of Route 66, where all its bad turns, gimpy gift shops, and predatory mechanics are forgotten in favor of a smiley face on the Route 66 shield. Fredric Brown envisions this future taking place in the heart of a Route 66 city—Albuquerque (now one of the largest space ports on the globe). For prisoners along the Route 66 corridor in the twenty-third century, via jet and rocket, getting there is only half the fun—getting out wins the prize.

Mystery and pulp writer Fredric Brown lived in the desert Southwest in Tucson, Arizona. Between the years 1947 and 1963, he published no fewer than twenty-nine novels, including The Far Cry (1987) and Night of the Jabberwock (1984). His work has been widely adapted for film and television.

C all him Crag; it was the name he was using and it will serve as well as any name. He was a smuggler and a thief and a killer. He'd been a spaceman once and had a metal hand to show for it. That, and a taste for exotic liquors and a strong aversion for work. Work would have been futile for him in any case; he would have had to work a week, at anything but crime, to buy a single binge on even the cheapest of the nepenthes that alone made life worth living. He knew good from evil but cared not a grain of Martian sand for either of them. He was not lonely for he had made himself self-sufficient by hating everyone.

Especially now, because they had him. And of all places here in Albuquerque, the center of the Federation and the toughest spot on five planets to beat a rap. Albuquerque, where justice was more crooked than crime, where a criminal didn't have a chance unless he belonged to the machine. Independent operators were not wanted and did not last long. He should never have come here, but he'd been tipped to a sure thing and had taken a chance . . .

There was only one question left, and that was whether they'd give him twenty in the penal colony on bleak Callisto or whether they'd send him to the psycher.

He sat on the cot in his cell and wondered which would happen. It made a big difference. Life in the penal colony might turn out to be better than no life at all and there would always be the chance, however slender, of escape. But the thought of the psycher was intolerable. Before he'd let them send him to the psycher, he decided, he'd kill himself or get himself killed trying to escape.

Death was something you could look in the face and laugh at. But not the psycher. Not the way Crag looked at it. The electric chair of a few centuries before merely killed you; the psycher did something much worse than that. It adjusted you, unless it drove you crazy. Statistically, one time out of nine it drove you stark mad, and for this reason it was used only in extreme cases, for crimes that would have been punishable by death back in the days of capital punishment. And even for such crimes, including nephthin possession, it was not mandatory; the judge chose between it and the alternative maximum sentence of twenty years on Callisto. Crag shuddered at the thought that if the psycher ever were perfected, if that one chance out of nine of being lucky were eliminated, it would probably be made mandatory for much lesser crimes.

When the psycher worked, it made you normal. It made you normal by removing from your mind all the memories and experiences which had led you into aberration from the norm. All your memories and experiences, the good ones as well as the bad.

After the psycher, you started from scratch as far as personality was concerned. You remembered your skills; you knew how to talk and feed yourself, and if you'd known how to use a slide rule or play a flute you still knew how to use a slide rule or play a flute.

But you didn't remember your name unless they told you. And you didn't remember the time you were tortured for three days and two nights on Venus before the rest of the crew found you and took you away from the animated vegetables who didn't like meat in any form and particularly in human form. You didn't remember the time you were spacemad or the time you had to go nine days without water. You didn't remember anything that had ever happened to you.

You started from scratch, a different person . . .

A voice from a grill in the ceiling of the cell said, "Your trial has been called for fourteen hours. That is ten minutes from now. Be ready."

Crag glanced upward and made a rude noise at the grill. Since it was strictly a one-way communicator, the grill paid no attention.

Crag walked over to the window and stood looking down at the vast sprawling city of Albuquerque, third largest city in the solar system, second largest city on Earth. Running diagonally off to the southeast he could see the bright ribbon of the shuttlejet track that led to Earth's largest spaceport, forty miles away.

The window was not barred but the transparent plastic of the pane was tough stuff. He could probably batter it out with his left hand but would need wings to continue an escape in that direction. His cell was on the top floor of Fedjude, the Federation Judicial Building, thirty stories high, the wall sheer and the windows flush. He could only commit suicide that way, and suicide could wait, as long as there was even a chance of getting the penal colony instead of the psycher.

He hated it, that corrupt city, worse in its way than Mars City, the vice city of the solar system. Albuquerque was not a fleshpot, but it was the center of intrigue between the Guilds and the Gilded. Politics rampant upon a field of muck, and everybody, except the leaders, caught in the middle, no matter which side they supported or even if they tried to remain neutral.

Through the windowpane, Craig caught the faint silver flash of a spaceship coming in, heard dimly the distant thunder of its jets.

BRAVE NEW WORLD

ALDOUS HUXLEY

− 2547 −

In Aldous Huxley's fantasy of the twenty-sixth century, the world has one government, and all the earth's children are born in hatcheries. In this novel, the first to address human cloning, children are genetically coded at birth and socially conditioned to take up their assigned, hierarchical roles in society. Only the Savages, a cult of primitives in the mountains of New Mexico, north of Route 66, still reproduce the old-fashioned way. This practice brings tourists of the intrepid sort, who arrive there in rockets from London that follow Route 66 and the old Santa Fe Trail. Bernard Marx journeys with his girlfriend, Lenina—no female version of Lenin—to savages depicted as outcasts. Their slumming expedition becomes a voyage of discovery into a twenty-sixth-century Heart of Darkness, out where the buffalo and automobiles roamed.

In 1932, Huxley imagined rockets "capable of flying any distance up to five thousand miles, and traveling along a radio beam precisely to their destination." The long day's journey from London to Santa Fe passes quickly under the influence of the all-persuasive narcotic Soma: "a gram is better than a damn." Huxley foresaw a technocratic tyranny, where a "narco-hypnosis is more efficient than clubs or prisons." Whether or not this comes to pass, Brave New World was such a sensation that it was translated into twenty-eight languages.

The author of over sixty books, Aldous Leonard Huxley spent the last third of his life in California, where he wrote films, novels, plays, and essays.

The journey was quite uneventful. The Blue Pacific Rocket was two and a half minutes early at New Orleans, lost four minutes in a tornado over Texas, but flew into a favourable air current at Longitude 95 West, and was able to land at Santa Fé less than forty seconds behind schedule time.

"Forty seconds on a six and a half hour flight. Not so bad," Lenina conceded.

They slept that night at Santa Fé. The hotel was excellent—incomparably better, for example, than that horrible Aurora Bora Palace in which Lenina had suffered so much the previous summer. Liquid air, television, vibro-vacuum massage, radio, boiling caffeine solution, hot contraceptives, and eight different kinds of scent were laid on in every bedroom. The synthetic music plant was working as they entered the hall and left nothing to be desired. A notice in the lift announced that there were sixty Escalator-Squash-Racquet Courts in the hotel, and that Obstacle and Electro-magnetic Golf could both be played in the park.

"But it sounds simply too lovely," cried Lenina. "I almost wish we could stay here. Sixty Escalator-Squash Courts . . ."

"There won't be any in the Reservation," Bernard warned her. "And no scent, no television, no hot water even. If you feel you can't stand it, stay here till I come back."

Lenina was quite offended. "Of course I can stand it. I only said it was lovely here because . . . well, because progress is lovely, isn't it?" . . .

A message from the porter announced that, at the Warden's orders, a Reservation Guard had come round with a plane and was waiting on the roof of the hotel. They went up at once.

An octoroon in a Gamma-green uniform saluted and proceeded to recite the morning's programme.

A bird's-eye view of ten or a dozen of the principal pueblos, then a landing for lunch in the valley of Malpais. The rest-house was comfortable there, and up at the pueblo the savages would probably be celebrating their summer festival. It would be the best place to spend the night.

They took their seats in the plane and set off. Ten minutes later they were crossing the frontier that separated civilization from savagery. Uphill and down, across the deserts of salt or sand, through forests, into the violet depths of canyons, over crag and peak and table-topped mesa, the fence marched on and on, irresistibly the straight line, the geometrical symbol of triumphant human purpose . . .

"Malpais," explained the pilot, as Bernard stepped out. "This is the rest-house. And there's a dance this afternoon at the pueblo. He'll take you there." He pointed to the sullen young savage. "Funny, I expect." He grinned. "Everything they do is funny." And with that he climbed into the plane and started the engines. "Back to-morrow. And remember," he added reassuringly to Lenina, "they're perfectly tame; savages won't do you any harm. They've got enough experience of gas bombs to know that they mustn't play any tricks." Still laughing, he threw the helicopter screws into gear, accelerated, and was gone.

The mesa was like a ship becalmed in a strait of lion-coloured dust. The channel wound between precipitous banks, and slanting from one wall to the other across the valley ran a streak of green—the river and its fields. On the prow of that stone ship in the center of the strait, and seemingly a part of it, a shaped and geometrical outcrop of the naked rock, stood the pueblo of Malpais. Block above block, each story smaller than the one below, the tall houses rose like stepped and amputated pyramids into the blue sky . . .

"Queer," said Lenina. "Very queer." It was her ordinary word of condemnation. "I don't like it."

Santa Monica, California

A SELECT ROUTE 66
BIBLIOGRAPHY

GENERAL INTEREST

Benson, Sara. *Lonely Planet Road Trip: Route 66.* Oakland, CA: Lonely Planet Publications, 2003.

Bischoff, Matt. *Life in the Past Lane: The Route 66 Experience.* Tucson, AZ: University of Arizona Press, 2006.

Brown, Polly, and Jane Bernard. *American Route 66: Home on the Road.* Santa Fe, NM: Museum of New Mexico Press, 2003.

Buckley, Patricia. *Route 66: Remnants.* Privately printed, 1988.

Cassity, Michael. *Route 66 Corridor National Historical Context Survey.* Santa Fe, NM: National Park Service Route 66 Corridor Preservation Program, 2007.

Cobb, James. *West on 66.* New York: Thomas Dunne Books, 1999.

Freeth, Nick. *Traveling Route 66.* Norman, OK: University of Oklahoma Press, 2001.

Kaszynski, William. *Route 66: Images of America's Main Street.* Jefferson, NC: McFarland & Company, Inc., 2003.

Knowles, Drew. *Route 66 Adventure Handbook.* 3rd ed. Santa Monica, CA: Santa Monica Press, 2006.

Krim, Arthur, and Denis Wood, eds. *Route 66: Iconography of the American Highway.* Staunton, VA: Center for American Places, 2006.

Krump, Spencer. *Route 66: America's First Main Street.* Corona Del Mar, CA: Zeta Publishers, 1996.

Martin, Norman. *Up on Route 66.* Searcy, AR: Martian Press, 2000.

Miller, Henry. *The Air-Conditioned Nightmare.* New York: New Directions, 1945.

Moore, Bob, and Rich Cunningham. *The Complete Atlas to Route 66.* Laughlin, NV: Route 66 Magazine, 2003.

Moore, Bob, and Rich Cunningham. *The Complete Guide to Route 66.* Laughlin, NV: Route 66 Magazine, 2003.

National Historic Route 66 Federation. *Route 66 Dining and Lodging Guide.* 12th ed. Lake Arrowhead, CA, 2006.

National Park Service. *Route 66: Illinois, Missouri, Kansas, Oklahoma, Texas, New Mexico, Arizona, California.* Denver, CO: National Park Service, Denver Service Center, 1995.

Repp, Thomas A. *Route 66: Empires of Amusement.* Lynnwood, WA: Mock Turtle Press, 1999.

Repp, Thomas A. *Route 66: The Romance of the West.* Lynnwood, WA: Mock Turtle Press, 2002.

Rittenhouse, Jack D. *A Guide Book to Highway 66.* A facsimile of the 1946 first edition. Albuquerque, NM: University of New Mexico Press, 1989.

Robinson, Jon. *Route 66: Lives on the Road.* Osceola, WI: MBI Publishing, 2001.

Robson, Ellen, and Diane Halicki. *Haunted Highway: The Spirits of Route 66.* Laughlin, NV: Golden West Publishers, 1999.

Rooker, Oliver. *Riding the Travel Bureau.* Canton, OK: Memoir Publishing, 1994.

Rosin, James. *Route 66, the Television Series: 1960–1964.* Philadelphia, PA: Autumn Road Co., 2007.

Rugh, Susan Sessions. *Are We There Yet? The Golden Age of American Family Vacations.* Lawrence, KS: University Press of Kansas, 2008.

Sanders, William. *A Death on 66.* New York: St. Martin's Press, 1994.

Scott, Quinta. *Along Route 66.* Norman, OK: University of Oklahoma Press, 2000.

Steinbeck, John. *The Grapes of Wrath.* New York: Viking Press, 1939.

Strickland, Elizabeth. *Route 66 to the Fields of California.* Tallahassee, FL: Clark Publishing, 2002.

Taylor, Paul. *Route 66 Place Names.* Laughlin, NV: Route 66 Magazine, 2006.

Teague, Tom. *Searching for 66.* 2nd ed. Springfield, IL: Samizdat Press, 1991.

Wallis, Michael. *Route 66: The Mother Road.* 75th Anniversary Edition. New York: St. Martin's Griffin, 2001.

Wickline, David. *Images of 66.* Westerville, OH: Roadhouse 66, LLC, 2006.

Witzel, Michael Karl. *Route 66.* Ann Arbor, MI: Lowe & B. Hould Publishers, 1996.

Witzel, Michael Karl. *Route 66 Remembered.* Osceola, WI: Motorbooks International, 1996.

MONOGRAPHS, THESES, AND MAPS

Dunaway, David King. *Across the Tracks: A Route 66 Story.* Albuquerque, NM: Dept. of English, University of New Mexico, 2002.

Ellis, Don R. "The Economic Influence of U.S. 66 and I.H. 40 Between Oklahoma City and Texola, Oklahoma." MA thesis, University of Oklahoma, 1969.

Hodgman, Leonard. "Roadside Utilization along Selected Bypass Sites: US Route 66 in Illinois." MA thesis, Illinois State University, 1957.

National Park Service. *Route 66 Corridor*. Washington, DC: NPS, 1994.

ProMap. *Historic Route 66*. Palmdale, CA: ProMap, 1996.

Puzo, Rita A. "Route 66: A Ghost Road Geography." MA thesis, California State University at Fullerton, 1988.

Ross, Jim, and Jerry McClanahan. *Here It Is: The Route 66 Map Series*. Arcadia, OK: Ghost Town Press, 2000.

Ryburn-LaMonte, Terri. "Route 66, 1926 to Present: The Road as Local History." PhD dissertation, Illinois State University, 1999.

Shrade, Ida M. "The Sequent Occupation of the Rancho Azusa de Duarte." PhD dissertation, University of Chicago, 1948.

Thomas, J. F., ed. "Get Your Kix on Route 66." *Bulletin of the Illinois Geographical Society* 38, no. 2 (January 1996).

Waldmire, Robert. *State Maps of Route 66*. Self-published, 1983.

HISTORICAL BACKGROUND

Dedek, Peter. *Hip to the Trip*. Albuquerque, NM: University of New Mexico Press, 2007.

DeKehoe, Joe. *The Silence and the Sun: An Historical Account of People, Places, and Events on Old Route 66 and Railroad Communities in the Eastern Mojave Desert, California*. Bakersfield, CA: Trails End Publishing Company.

Dodge, Bertha S. *The Road West*. Albuquerque, NM: University of New Mexico Press, 1980.

Fergusson, Harvey. *In Those Days*. Boston, MA: Gregg Press, 1978.

Goddard, Stephen B. *Getting There*. New York: Basic Books, 1994.

Gregory, James N. *American Exodus: The Dust Bowl Migration and Okie Culture in California*. New York: Oxford University Press, 1989.

Hofsommer, Donovan, L. *Railroads in Oklahoma*. Oklahoma City, OK: Oklahoma Historical Society, 1977.

Jackson, W. Turrentine. *Wagon Roads West*. Lincoln, NE: University of Nebraska, 1964.

Kastner, Charles B. *Bunion Derby: The 1928 Footrace Across America*. Albuquerque, NM: University of New Mexico Press, 2007.

Lamar, Howard Roberts. *The Far Southwest: 1846–1912, A Territorial History*. New York: W. W. Norton & Company, 1970.

Lowe, Joseph. *The National Old Trails Highway*. Kansas City, KS: Old Trails Road Association, 1925.

Meinig, D.W. *Southwest: Three Peoples in Geographical Change 1600–1970*. New York: Oxford University Press, 1971.

Myrick, David F. *New Mexico's Railroads*. Golden, CO: Colorado Railroad Historical Foundation, 1970.

Patton, Phil. *Open Road: A Celebration of the American Highway*. New York: Touchstone, 1986.

Price, Sean. *Route 66: America's Road*. Chicago, IL: Raintree, 2008.

Riegel, Robert Edgar. *The Story of the Western Railroads*. New York: Macmillan Company, 1926.

Thomas, D.H. *The Southwestern Indian Detours*. Phoenix, AZ: Hunter Publishing Co., 1978.

Thomas, Jones. *The Bunion Derby*. Oklahoma City, OK: Southwest Heritage Books, 1980.

Waters, L. L. *Steel Trails to Santa Fe*. Lawrence, KS: University of Kansas Press, 1950.

Webb, Walter Prescott. *The Great Plains*. New York: Grossett and Dunlap, 1931.

Williams, Geoff. *C. C. Pyle's Amazing Foot Race: The True Story of the 1928 Coast-to-Coast Run Across America*. New York: Rodale Books, 2007.

Winther, Oscar Osburn. *The Transportation Frontier: Trans-Mississippi West, 1865–1890*. New York: Holt, Rinehart and Winston, 1964.

Witzel, Michael Karl. *Legendary Route 66: A Journey Through Time Along America's Mother Road*. St. Paul, MN: Voyageur Press, 2007.

SELECTED REGIONAL WORKS

Anders, Mary Ann, ed. *Route 66 in Oklahoma: An Historic Preservation Survey*. Stillwater, OK: Oklahoma State History Department, 1984.

Clark, David. *Exploring Route 66 in Chicagoland*. Chicago, IL: Windy City Road Warrior, 2006.

Clark, David. *Route 66 in Chicago*. Chicago, IL: Arcadia Publishing, 2007.

Curtis, Skip. *The Missouri U.S. 66 Tour Book*. Lake St. Louis, MO: Curtis Enterprises, 1994.

Davies, Vivian, and Davin Kuna. *California's Route 66*. La Verne, CA: California Route 66 Association, 1994.

Duncan, Glenn. *Route 66 in California*. San Francisco, CA: Arcadia Publishing, 2005.

Harwell, Joanna, ed. *Oldham County Remembers Route 66*. Vega, TX: Oldham County Chamber of Commerce, 1997.

Kammer, David. *The Historical and Architectural Resources of Route 66 Through New Mexico*. Santa Fe, NM: New Mexico Historic Preservation Division, 1992.

Kammer, David. *Route 66 Through New Mexico: Re-Survey Report*. Santa Fe, NM: New Mexico Office of Cultural Affairs, Historic Preservation Office, 2003.

Keene, David. *Illinois Historic Route 66 Corridor Study.* Chicago, IL: Illinois State Office of Historic Preservation, 1994.

Mangum, Richard, and Shirley G. Mangum. *Route 66 Across Arizona.* Flagstaff, AZ: Hexagon Press, 2001.

Meacham, Maryjo. *Route 66 and Associated Historic Resources in Oklahoma.* National Register of Historic Places. Multiple Property Documentation Form. Norman, OK, 1992.

National Park Service. *Historic Resources of Route 66 in Kansas.* Washington, DC: NPS, 1986.

Noe, Sally. *66 Sights on Route 66.* Gallup, NM: Gallup Development Group, 1992.

Piotrowski, Scott. *Finding the End of the Mother Road: Route 66 in LA County.* Pasadena, CA: 66 Publications, 2003.

Price, Byron B., and Frederick W. Rathjen. *The Golden Spread: An Illustrated History of Amarillo and the Texas Panhandle.* Northridge, CA: Windsor Publications, 1986.

Ross, Jim. *Oklahoma Route 66.* 2nd ed. Arcadia, OK: Ghost Town Press, 2001.

Schneider, Jill. *Route 66 Across New Mexico.* Albuquerque, NM: University of New Mexico Press, 1991.

Trew, Delbert. *Notes and Tales on Texas's Old Route 66.* Alanreed, TX: Self-published, 1990.

Weiss, John. *Traveling the New Historic Route 66 in Illinois.* Frankfort, IL: A.O. Motivation Programs, 1998.

SELECTED ORAL HISTORY PUBLICATIONS

Dunaway, David King. *Route 66 Oral History: A Manual.* Santa Fe, NM: National Park Service, Route 66 Corridor Preservation Program, 2007.

Dunaway, David King, ed. *Oral History Reader.* Santa Fe, NM: National Park Service, Route 66 Corridor Preservation Program, 2003.

Dunaway, David King, and Willa K. Baum, ed. *Oral History: An Interdisciplinary Anthology.* 2nd ed. Lanham, MD: Rowman & Littlefield, 1996.

Neuenschwander, John A. *Oral History and the Law.* Carlisle, PA: Oral History Association, 2002.

Ritchie, Donald A. *Doing Oral History: A Practical Guide.* 2nd ed. New York: Oxford University Press, 2003.

Sommer, Barbara, W., and Mary Kay Quinlan. *The Oral History Manual.* Walnut Creek, CA: AltaMira Press and Rowman and Littlefield, 2002.

Wood, Linda P. *Oral History: Projects in Your Classroom.* Carlisle, PA: Oral History Association, 2001.

CREDITS

On the Western Tour with Washington Irving: The Journal and Letters of Count de Pourtalès. *Edited by George F. Spaulding. Translated by Seymour Feiler. Norman: University of Oklahoma Press, 1968.*

"One Night in the Red Dog Saloon," by Hal G. Evarts, Jr. *Reprinted by permission of Don Congdon Associates, Inc. Copyright © 1953 by the Curtis Publishing Company, renewed 1981 by Hal G. Evarts, Jr.*

"Too Many Midnights," by Carolyn Wheat. *From* Murder on Route 66, *edited by Carolyn Wheat (New York: Berkley Prime Crime, 1998). Used with permission.*

"The Lost Boy," by Thomas Wolfe. *Used with permission of the Estate of Thomas Wolfe.*

"The Boy: Okie Passage on Route 66," by Jay Smith. *From* The Boy: Okie Passage on Route 66 *(Boca Raton, FL: Tall Cotton Press, 1992).*

"Blind Corner," by David August. *From* Murder on Route 66, *edited by Carolyn Wheat (New York: Berkley Prime Crime, 1998). Used with permission.*

"West on 66," by James H. Cobb. *From* West on 66: A Mystery *(New York: Thomas Dunne Books, 1999). Used with permission.*

"The Autobiography of Will Rogers," by Will Rogers. *Excerpted from* The Autobiography of Will Rogers, *edited by Donald Day. Copyright 1949 by Rogers Company; copyright renewed © 1977 by Donald Day and Beth Day.*

"*Wild Boy of the Road,*" by Karen Hesse. From Out of the Dust *by Karen Hesse. Copyright © 1997 by Karen Hesse. Reprinted by permission of Scholastic Inc.*

"*The Negro Motorist Green Book,*" by Victor H. Green. From The Negro Motorist Green Book: An International Travel Guide, U.S.A., Alaska, Bermuda, Mexico, Canada *(New York: Victor H. Green & Co., 1949).*

"'*53 Buick,*" by Gary Phillips. From Murder on Route 66, *edited by Carolyn Wheat (New York: Berkley Prime Crime, 1998). Used with permission.*

"*Mining Along 66,*" by Raymond Wierth and Joe Miller. From *interviews recorded and transcribed in 1980. Used with permission of the Mojave Museum of History & Arts.*

"*Hot Saturday,*" by Harvey Fergusson. From Hot Saturday *by Harvey Fergusson (New York: Knopf, 1926). Used with permission.*

"*The Thin Mountain Air,*" by Paul Horgan. From The Thin Mountain Air *by Paul Horgan (New York: Farrar, Straus and Giroux, 1977). Used with permission.*

"*The Grapes of Wrath,*" by John Steinbeck. *Excerpted from chapter twelve of* The Grapes of Wrath *by John Steinbeck, copyright 1939, renewed © 1967 by John Steinbeck. Used by permission of Viking Penguin, a division of Penguin Group (USA) Inc.*

"*The Hitch-Hiker,*" by Lucille Fletcher. *Copyright © 1947, 1952, renewed 1980 by Lucille Fletcher. Reprinted by permission of William Morris Agency, LLC, on behalf of the author.*

"*Ceremony,*" by Leslie Marmon Silko. From Ceremony *by Leslie Marmon Silko, copyright © 1977 by Leslie Silko. Used by permission of Viking Penguin, a division of Penguin Group (USA) Inc.*

"*The Air-Conditioned Nightmare,*" by Henry Miller. *Excerpted from* The Air-Conditioned Nightmare *by Henry Miller, copyright © 1945 by New Directions Publishing Corp. Reprinted by permission of New Directions Publishing Corp.*

"*Gunslinger,*" by Ed Gorman. From The Californians: The Best of the West, *edited by Bill Pronzini and Martin H. Greenberg (New York: Ballantine Books, 1989). Used with permission.*

"*The High Window,*" by Raymond Chandler. From The High Window *by Raymond Chandler, copyright 1942 by Raymond Chandler and renewed 1970 by*

Helga Greene, Executrix of the Estate of Raymond Chandler. Used by permission of Alfred A. Knopf, a division of Random House, Inc.

"Blue Time," by Earlene Fowler. From Murder on Route 66, edited by Carolyn Wheat (New York: Berkley Prime Crime, 1998). Used with permission.

"Sleep in the Mojave Desert," by Sylvia Plath. From Crossing the Water by Sylvia Plath, copyright © 1962 by Sylvia Plath. Reprinted by permission of HarperCollins Publishers. Originally appeared in Harper's Magazine.

"Some Dreamers of the Golden Dream," by Joan Didion. From Slouching Towards Bethlehem by Joan Didion (New York: Simon and Schuster, 1961). Used with permission.

"Sleeping Beauty" by Ross MacDonald. From Sleeping Beauty by Ross Mac-Donald, copyright © 1973 by Ross MacDonald. Used by permission of Alfred A. Knopf, a division of Random House, Inc.

"Rogue in Space," by Fredric Brown. From Rogue in Space by Fredric Brown (New York: E. P. Dutton & Company, Inc., 1957). Used with permission.

"Brave New World," by Aldous Huxley. Exerpt from Brave New World by Aldous Huxley, 117–121. Copyright 1932, renewed © 1960 by Aldous Huxley. Reprinted by permission of HarperCollins Publishers.

VISUALS

"Map of Old Route 66" by Bob Waldmire, 1992.

ORAL HISTORIES

The following excerpts are from oral histories recorded by David King Dunaway in the decade 1998–2008.

Dave Edmunds, "Buffalo Hunting on Route 66"
Michael Amundson, "Railroaders' Route 66"
Man Susanyatame, "Recalling Route 66's Trail of Tears"
Greg Malak, "Working with Will"
Lance Henson, "Back Road 66"
Edmond Threatt, "Black on 66"

Michael Wallis, "Mr. Route 66"
Robert M. Davis, "Kicking 66"
Delbert Trew, "On Route 66 in Texas"
Stanley Marsh III, "Cadillac Ranch"
Mary Toya, "Laguna Exile"
Rudolfo Anaya, "Hispanic on Route 66"
Louis Owens, "Indian Farm-Workers on 66"
Ry Cooder, "The Music of 66"
Robert Ervin, "Soul in the Desert"
Peter Friedman, "A Rocket Scientist Looks at Route 66's Future"

ACKNOWLEDGMENTS

This book has taken four years to produce, and during that time a number of editorial assistants at the University of New Mexico contributed greatly: Felicia Karas, Kristen Cole, Stephanie Spong, Nic Albonico, and Nora Hickey. My thanks to all of these—plus my hopes that their advanced education will bring them satisfaction in life.

My editors at the University of Texas Press, William Bishel and Casey Kittrell, were most supportive and deserve recognition. In addition, my literary agent, Loretta Barrett, was most supportive.

My ultimate thanks go to the many individuals who allowed themselves and their work to be reprinted here or recorded as oral history, and to the students who helped transcribe and index these interviews. I hope all these accounts someday find their way into a major oral history collection; for too long Route 66 has been a locus of nostalgia, but these residents and travelers along 66 tell it like it is!

ABOUT THE AUTHOR

David King Dunaway was born and raised in Greenwich Village in New York City. He attended the University of Aix-en-Provence, France, and the University of Wisconsin, with graduate studies at the University of California Berkeley, where he received Berkeley's first Ph.D. in American Studies. At the University of New Mexico, Dr. Dunaway teaches nonfiction, and he has served as a Fulbright Senior Lecturer at the University of Nairobi, the National University of Colombia, and the University of Copenhagen. He is currently Distinguished Professor of Broadcasting at San Francisco State University.

Dr. Dunaway's biography *How Can I Keep From Singing? The Ballad of Pete Seeger* won the American Society of Composers, Authors, and Publishers' Deems Taylor Award for excellence in writing about American music. His articles about American culture have appeared in publications ranging from *The Virginia Quarterly* to the *New York Times*. Dr. Dunaway is also an award-winning producer of radio documentaries and podcasts on literary and historical topics, such as *Across the Tracks: A Route 66 Story*, a three-hour public radio series. His website is www.davidkdunaway.com.

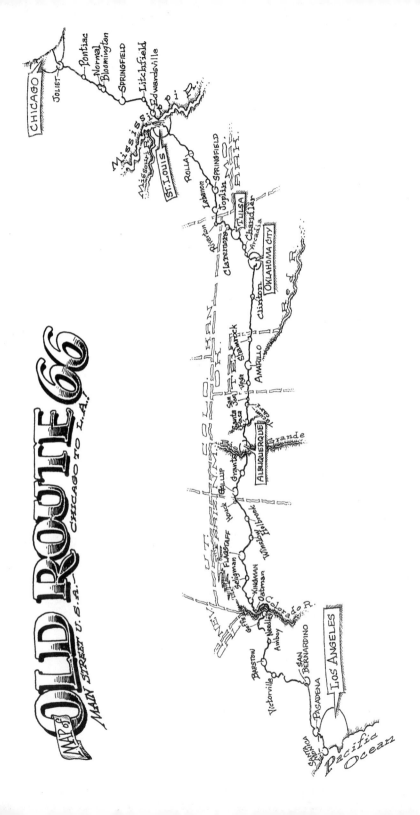

MAP OF **OLD ROUTE 66**

MAIN STREET U.S.A.!

CHICAGO TO L.A.!

CHICAGO
Joliet
Pontiac
Normal
Bloomington
Springfield
Litchfield
Edwardsville
Mississippi R.
Missouri R.
ST. LOUIS
Rolla
Lebanon
Riverton
Claremore
Springfield MO.
Joplin
TULSA
Chandler
Arcadia
OKLAHOMA CITY
Clinton
Red R.
Shamrock
Vega
AMARILLO
Santa Rosa
Tucumcari
Grants
ALBUQUERQUE
Grande
Gallup
Houck
Flagstaff
Seligman
Kingman
Oatman
Winslow
Holbrook
Colorado R.
Gffs
Needles
Amboy
Barstow
Victorville
San Bernardino
Pasadena
LOS ANGELES
SANTA MONICA
Pacific Ocean

ILLINOIS
MISSOURI
KANSAS
OKLAHOMA
TEXAS
NEW MEXICO
ARIZONA
CALIFORNIA